PATHWAYS TO PROFICIENCY

implementing evidence-based grading

troy   mark   anthony r.   eric

GOBBLE   ONUSCHECK   REIBEL   TWADELL

Solution Tree | Press

a division of
Solution Tree

MW01090109

555 North Morton Street
Bloomington, IN 47404
800.733.6786 (toll free) / 812.336.7700
FAX: 812.336.7790

email: info@SolutionTree.com
SolutionTree.com

Visit **go.SolutionTree.com/assessment** to download the free reproducibles in this book.

Printed in the United States of America

21 20 19 18 17   2 3 4 5

Library of Congress Cataloging-in-Publication Data

Names: Gobble, Troy, author.
Title: Pathways to proficiency : implementing evidence-based grading / Troy
    Gobble, Mark Onuscheck, Anthony R. Reibel, and Eric Twadell.
Description: Bloomington, IN : Solution Tree Press, [2017] | Includes
    bibliographical references and index.
Identifiers: LCCN 2016053171 | ISBN 9781942496137 (perfect bound)
Subjects: LCSH: Grading and marking (Students) | Educational tests and
    measurements--Methodology.
Classification: LCC LB3060.37 .G64 2017 | DDC 371.27/2--dc23 LC record available at https://lccn
    .loc.gov/2016053171

Solution Tree
Jeffrey C. Jones, CEO
Edmund M. Ackerman, President

Solution Tree Press
President and Publisher: Douglas M. Rife
Editorial Director: Tonya Maddox Cupp
Managing Production Editor: Caroline Weiss
Senior Production Editor: Christine Hood
Senior Editor: Amy Rubenstein
Copy Chief: Sarah Payne-Mills
Copy Editors: Miranda Addonizio and Ashante K. Thomas
Proofreader: Jessi Finn
Text and Cover Designer: Rian Anderson
Editorial Assistants: Jessi Finn and Kendra Slayton

The authors intend to donate all of their royalties to the Stevenson High School Foundation.

BLOOM'S
Growth Mindset
PBL
Personal Data Notebook

To Danielle; thanks for your love, patience, and support.
—Troy Gobble

To Dr. Bernard T. Hart, a life's guide and a great educator.
—Mark Onuscheck

To my wife for her incredible patience and unwavering support.
—Anthony R. Reibel

For Mom; thank you for teaching me what hard work and perseverance look like.
—Eric Twadell

Acknowledgments

A long time ago, the old Yankee Stadium was called "The House That Ruth Built." We don't think it would stretch our credibility in the least to suggest that Adlai E. Stevenson High School is "The House That Doc Built." Stevenson High School has been noted as the most recognized and celebrated school in America and the birthplace of the professional learning community (PLC) movement. Under the leadership of former principal and superintendent Rick DuFour (also known as Doc), Stevenson has become a model of education reform and a lighthouse to those looking to implement best practices and create a PLC culture in their own schools. Although Rick retired from Stevenson in June 2002, we owe him great gratitude, and his legacy lives on in the culture of continuous improvement that permeates every aspect of our school's daily life. The PLC process is well embedded into the DNA of our school culture.

We feel blessed to be working at a school that has been on the leading edge of reform for more than twenty-five years, and Solution Tree has been sharing our stories along the way. Many thanks to all our friends at Solution Tree, including Jeff Jones, Ed Ackerman, Douglas Rife, and Shannon Ritz. Claudia Wheatley has been our champion and advocate, continually pushing us to clarify our thinking about *proficiency* and share the next chapter in our school's story of continuous improvement. And last, but most certainly not least, we are grateful for our new friend and editor Christine Hood, who has been supportive and patient as we tried to translate our experiences with evidence-based grading in our school into a story that will guide and help other schools and teachers create new and improved evidence-based grading and reporting systems.

Stevenson's administrative team works relentlessly to ensure that faculty and staff have the tools to guarantee high levels of learning for all students, and the team comprises passionate protectors of our school's mission, vision, and values. Likewise, we must thank Adlai E. Stevenson High School District 125's board of education for its continued service and support: Steve Frost, Gary Gorson, Sunit Jain, Bruce Lubin, Terry Moons, Merv Roberts, and Dave Weisberg. Our board is unrelenting in its expectation that we improve each year as we move closer to our mission of *success for every student.*

Finally, and most important, we owe special thanks to the Stevenson High School faculty who are leading the evidence-based grading journey. As we endeavor to build on the strong foundation of excellence here at Stevenson, we find that if we are truly going to realize our vision and values, we need to upend the traditional grading and reporting system used at Stevenson and across the United States for many years. To our amazement, our faculty have tackled the challenge head-on, rethinking and reshaping grading and reporting practices.

While it certainly isn't easy work, our faculty have demonstrated a steadfast commitment to improving teaching and learning conditions for students that is truly inspiring. This book represents faculty members' journey through implementing evidence-based grading and reporting. We stand in awe of their willingness to set aside personal interests, convenience, and individual autonomy to do the hard work of creating an evidence-based grading and reporting system that actually helps and supports student learning and achievement. We are merely their storytellers.

Solution Tree Press would like to thank the following reviewers:

Tyler Auer
Mathematics Teacher
Fay School
Southborough, Massachusetts

Jill Maraldo
Associate Principal for Instruction
Buffalo Grove High School
Buffalo Grove, Illinois

Tyler Hartl
Principal
Sagewood Elementary School
Casper, Wyoming

Jim Pardun
Mathematics Teacher
Vernon Hills High School
Vernon Hills, Illinois

Jodi Leimkuehler
Business and Technology Teacher
Solon High School
Solon, Iowa

The authors intend to donate all their royalties to the Stevenson High School Foundation.

Visit **go.SolutionTree.com/assessment** to download the free reproducibles in this book.

Table of Contents

Chapter 3
Insight 71

Chapter 4
Evaluation 99

Chapter 5
Elaboration 125

About the Authors

Troy Gobble is principal of Adlai E. Stevenson High School, in Lincolnshire, Illinois. He previously served as assistant principal for teaching and learning at Stevenson. Troy taught science for eighteen years and served as the science department chair for eight years at Riverside Brookfield High School, in Riverside, Illinois.

The United States Department of Education (USDE) describes Stevenson as the most recognized and celebrated school in America, and Stevenson is one of only three schools to win the USDE National Blue Ribbon Award on four occasions. Stevenson was one of the first comprehensive schools that the USDE designated a New American High School as a model of successful school reform, and it is repeatedly cited as one of America's top high schools and the birthplace of the Professional Learning Communities at Work™ process.

Troy holds a master of science degree in educational administration from Benedictine University, a master of science degree in natural sciences (physics) from Eastern Illinois University, and a bachelor's degree in secondary science education from the University of Illinois at Urbana–Champaign.

Mark Onuscheck is director of curriculum, instruction, and assessment at Adlai E. Stevenson High School, in Lincolnshire, Illinois. He is a former English teacher and director of communication arts. As director of curriculum, instruction, and assessment, Mark works with academic divisions around professional learning, articulation, curricular and instructional revision, evaluation, assessment, social-emotional learning, technologies, and Common Core implementation. He is also an adjunct professor at DePaul University.

Mark was awarded the Quality Matters Star Rating for his work in online teaching. He helps build curriculum and instructional practices for TimeLine Theatre's arts integration program for Chicago Public Schools. Additionally, he is a National Endowment for the Humanities' grant recipient and a member of the Association for Supervision and Curriculum Development, the National Council of Teachers of English, the International Reading Association, and Learning Forward.

Mark earned a bachelor's degree in English and classical studies from Allegheny College and a master's degree in teaching English from the University of Pittsburgh.

Anthony R. Reibel is director of assessment, research, and evaluation at Adlai E. Stevenson High School, in Lincolnshire, Illinois. He administers assessments, manages student achievement data, and oversees instructional practice. Anthony began his professional career as a technology specialist and entrepreneur. After managing several businesses, he became a Spanish teacher at Stevenson. He also served as a curricular team leader, core team leader, coach, and club sponsor.

In 2010, the Illinois Computing Educators named him Technology Educator of the Year for successfully integrating technology to support student learning. He is a member of the Association for Supervision and Curriculum Development, the Illinois Principals Association, Illinois Computing Educators, and the American Council on the Teaching of Foreign Languages.

Anthony earned a bachelor's degree in Spanish from Indiana University and master's degrees in curriculum and instruction and in educational leadership from Roosevelt University.

To learn more about Anthony's work, follow @areibel on Twitter.

Eric Twadell, PhD, is superintendent of Adlai E. Stevenson High School, in Lincolnshire, Illinois. He has been a social studies teacher, curriculum director, and assistant superintendent for leadership and organizational development.

Eric has coauthored several books and professional articles. As a dedicated professional learning community (PLC) practitioner, he has worked with state departments of education and local schools and districts throughout the United States to achieve school improvement and reform. An accessible and articulate authority on PLC concepts, Eric brings hands-on experience to his presentations and workshops.

In addition to his teaching and leadership roles, Eric has been involved in coaching numerous athletic teams and facilitating outdoor education and adventure travel programs. He is a member of many professional organizations.

Eric earned a master's degree in curriculum and instruction and a doctorate in educational leadership and policy studies from Loyola University Chicago.

To learn more about Eric's work, follow @ELT247365 on Twitter.

To book Troy Gobble, Mark Onuscheck, Anthony R. Reibel, or Eric Twadell for professional development, contact pd@SolutionTree.com.

Introduction

The Case for Evidence-Based Grading

We are believers in evidence-based grading, and we are not alone. Our students need a new, more effective grading system. We must rethink our traditional grading practices and build a new grading model that clarifies and communicates about student learning. When we take this step, we will engage in more effective conversations about teaching and learning, demonstrate evidence of learning for every student, drive innovative revisions to instructional practices, and gain more equitable consistency in our schools. Overall, we will build a clear working relationship among curriculum, instruction, and assessment.

This means hard work. This means getting specific about three things: (1) what we want students to know, understand, and do; (2) how we clearly state our performance expectations of students; and (3) why we must gather visible evidence of student learning so we can address the gaps in student achievement, build higher-quality instruction, and extend mastery over learning.

Past grading practices do not communicate specifically about learning. For this reason, educators struggle to engage in meaningful conversations that develop coherence around curriculum, instruction, and assessment. As a result, we often fumble over how to open crucial dialogue about what students know and what they do *not* know. Likewise, students sit through their classes unsure of expectations, and parents remain unclear about what their children need to do to succeed in school. Our work around evidence-based grading is focused on unifying the relationship among curriculum, instruction, and assessment so teachers and students can work together more explicitly on what student learning growth looks like.

Many of our best educators and researchers are working to improve discussions that confirm learning is taking place and all students are succeeding. These educators recognize the potential of grading practices to foster dialogue about teaching and learning and how that dialogue can help students progress in their learning. The following are a few headline statements that express the need to approach grading differently. In *Ahead of the Curve*, Ken O'Connor (2007a) says:

> Grading as it has been done traditionally promotes a culture of point accumulation, not learning. It encourages competition rather than collaboration. It often focuses on activities instead of results. It makes all assessment summative because everything students do gets a score, and every score ends up in the grade book. In many schools, grades have achieved "cult-like status" (Olson, 1995) where the grade is more important than whether or not students have learned anything. (pp. 127–128)

Douglas Reeves (2008) shares:

> The difference between failure and the honor roll often depends on the grading policies of the teacher. To reduce the failure rate, schools don't need a new curriculum, a new principal, new teachers, or new technology. They just need a better grading system. (p. 85)

The overriding desire for change is clear. We believe that we must create and support grading practices that reflect how well our students demonstrate what we want them to know, understand, and do. More important, we need students to know how to discuss learning expectations with their teachers, how to reflect on growth, and how to reach greater levels of proficiency and mastery.

This call for change is easier said than done. Shifting away from traditional grading practices is no easy task. Traditional grading practices have been around a long time—generations have been herded through schools branding students with grades that say very little about what they learned. Moving away from these grading practices will take thoughtful conversations, reflective revisions, and hard work.

In our own district, we have spent the better part of four years moving away from a grading model that went virtually unchanged from our school's opening in 1965. For nearly fifty years, we stuck with traditional grading practices that are most familiar to everyone in high schools and colleges—a model of counting points and percentages and putting a letter stamp on the student—A, B, C, D, or F.

For decades, we have agreed that these letters actually stand for something. We are here to question that long-standing agreement and share how we are working to clearly articulate what we expect students to know, understand, and do; how well we expect students to perform; and how we expect students to prove what they've learned with clear, explicit evidence.

Like most educators, we rarely questioned traditional practices despite what we know about growth in learning. These deeply embedded traditional practices continue to live in schools as they generalize descriptions of student performance and lump students into letter groups. "He's an 'A student'" and "She's a 'C student'" are comments that seem to have meaning in our schools, to our families, and in our judgments about what students know, understand, and do. These letter stamps operate like distinctions or labels. For better or worse, they denote each student's capacity and predict potential for success.

The truth is no one can really state what these letters stand for from classroom to classroom, school to school, or state to state. An A from Mr. Smith's classroom might be very different from an A in Ms. Garcia's classroom. An A in Mr. Smith's classroom might actually be a C in Ms. Garcia's classroom. Not to mention how an A in ninth-grade English in New York City might represent learning that is vastly different from an A in ninth-grade English in rural Alabama.

As we move forward in our efforts to change grading practices, we try to revise these long-standing generalities about how we grade and report student learning and, instead, report what our students know, understand, and are able to do. Breaking out of traditional grading practices that perpetuate generalities requires intentional conversations about teaching and learning. These conversations require meaningful changes in how we unify and articulate curriculum, instruction, and assessment. More important, these conversations are changing how teachers and students approach the learning process.

While we continue to implement a more effective grading model, two adages ring true: *No one size fits all* and *go slow to go fast*. In other words, when building a change in our grading practices, we believe (1) our teaching teams must collaborate and decide how best to implement shifts toward more communicative grading practices and (2) what is best for teaching and learning takes time to process.

For these reasons, we are not in a rush to make these changes overnight. Instead, we would rather have teachers unpack the value of these shifts in ways that support productive conversations with students and teams about curriculum, instruction, and assessment. Upending ineffective traditional grading is our goal. To do it, we've chosen to work mindfully and intentionally with teachers to support this change, answering their questions and developing their insights about teaching and learning.

A New Language: Evidence-Based Grading

In our own work and in the work we've observed in other schools, implementing either traditional grading or what is called *standards-based grading* often stalls the changes we need to make. While standards-based grading models have good intentions, many lead teachers back to ineffective traditions or grading practices that do little to open up the conversations we need to have about teaching and learning.

We propose shifting toward grading practices that focus on the *evidence* that students produce. As we emphasize in the book *Proficiency-Based Assessment* (Gobble, Onuscheck, Reibel, & Twadell, 2016), we must change the *language* we use for grading. We should grade the *evidence* students create to demonstrate what they know, understand, and can do. This is important as we change our approach to grading practices that reflect school shifts in curriculum, instruction, and assessment.

In this book, we assert that evidence of student learning must be the starting point of change. The evidence that students produce shows the relationship between their work and expected levels of proficiency. The conversations about teaching and learning then become much more dynamic and formative—every student gains clarity and perspective about how he or she can improve.

Merriam-Webster's Online Dictionary defines *evidence* as "something which shows that something else exists or is true" (Evidence, n.d.). This is the same way we look at grading student performance. We must examine the available body of facts and information to determine whether it proves student learning.

When curriculum teams make collaborative decisions about student evidence that demonstrate learning growth, we support more equitable learning environments across different classrooms. When these same teams calibrate and interpret evidence based on agreed-upon expectations, we guarantee accurate and consistent feedback across these classrooms. These two changes can remedy the often random, subjective, and arbitrary elements used to determine grades in traditional grading systems.

In order to implement evidence-based grading in their classrooms, teachers should focus on the elements we discuss in the following sections.

Curriculum Focuses on Proficiency-Based, Student-Friendly Learning Targets

Students should have access to a thoughtfully considered, well-designed, high-quality curriculum. While it is important that the curriculum has meaningful and relevant standards, it is just as important that it is written with student-friendly learning targets that challenge students daily. Students must be able to state what teachers are asking them to know, understand, and do. However, even clear learning targets are not enough. For those targets to be meaningful and useful learning tools, they must be *scaled for proficiency expectations*—in other words, we must be able to describe what proficiency looks like in terms of *mastery* and *needs improvement*.

In an evidence-based grading model, proficiency-based learning targets describe expectations for learning. They unpack standards for learning into specific, well-described statements of learning that make sense to students. In an evidence-based grading model, these descriptions then become a tool for learning; they state what students must learn and define what it means to reach or exceed learning proficiency. A well-written learning target makes sense to the student, and it clearly states performance expectations. Nothing is hidden about what a student must learn. We encourage teachers to use these learning targets as tools for growth and reflection. They help state the gradation of learning that a student must attain (Gobble et al., 2016).

Learning should be placed on a continuum of proficiency, not viewed as a scaffolded progression. Consider table I.1, which highlights the differences between a scaffolded learning progression and a proficiency-based gradation. Scaffolded learning identifies different skills students should learn in sequence, but it does not state an expectation for learning. However, proficiency-based gradation states what skills students are developing and how well they are meeting expectations.

Table I.1: Scaffolded Learning Progression Versus Proficiency-Based Gradation

Scaffolded Learning Progression	Proficiency-Based Gradation
The student can identify vocabulary terms.	The student can appropriately explain vocabulary terms in a written analysis using simple stated details from class.
The student can define vocabulary terms.	The student can accurately explain vocabulary terms in a written format using simple stated details from class.
The student can explain vocabulary terms.	The student can accurately explain vocabulary terms in a written format using complex stated details from class.
The student can analyze vocabulary terms.	The student can accurately explain vocabulary terms in a written format using creative and unique details.

Bloom's

A scaffolded learning process for students includes different skills: identify, define, explain, and analyze. A well-written learning target offers a gradation of learning within one directed skill—in this case, the ability to *explain*. The learning verb is fixed in proficiency-based gradations for learning; the verb does not change, but the degree to which the student is successful does.

In an evidence-based grading model, we know that the proficiency expectation is the most critical component of being able to classify student performance and ultimately give a grade. In *Proficiency-Based Assessment* (Gobble et al., 2016), we offer the following example of how a proficiency-based learning target is used for evidence-based grading. This example is a proficiency-based expectation for a unit of study on World War I:

> If we develop a gradation of learning and proficiency for our World War I target, it may look something like the following.
>
> 4—Using unique examples and opinions, *students will be able to effectively explain* the main political, economic, and social causes of World War I in a written analysis.
>
> 3—Using examples from class, students *will be able to effectively explain* the main political, economic, and social causes of World War I in a written analysis.
>
> 2—Using given definitions and terms, students *will be able to effectively explain* the main political, economic, and social causes of World War I in a written analysis.
>
> 1—Using a text, students *will be able to effectively explain* the main political, economic, and social causes of World War I in a written analysis. (pp. 19–20, emphasis added)

This particular proficiency scale pertains to a written analysis of WWI's causes and breaks down the expectations for learning. A learning gradation like this positions proficiency as a 3, which helps both the teacher and student develop a better picture of the student's growth and achievement in relation to a stated level of proficiency. Proficiency-based learning targets clarify the differences in student growth, providing students with clear descriptions of a learning destination: proficiency or mastery. This articulates how students are performing and where they have room for growth. A curriculum that supports evidence-based grading provides proficiency-based learning targets that clearly outline the intended competency or learning progression for students.

Instruction Focuses on Teacher and Student Reactions to Student-Produced Evidence

Teachers tend to intentionally plan traditional instructional sequences, deliver them in scaffolded segments, and verify their efficacy with either a formative or summative assessment. *Evidence-based instruction is much different.* It demands evidence. So, teachers must work with students to see the evidence of learning *before* they plan what direction the instruction takes from that point forward. In evidence-based grading, the sequence looks more like this: (1) observe and collect evidence of learning through formative assessment, (2) intentionally react by deploying instruction and engagement strategies, and (3) reflect on the state of learning and the potential for growth.

As we know from experience, traditional instructional techniques often promote shallow retention of material and can actually slow down the learning process for students. Figure I.1 shows the traditional instructional sequence: each small circle represents an instance of teaching and assessing a small component of what teachers ultimately expect of the student. The teacher moves deliberately from one small component to another before ultimately teaching and assessing students on the learning target. The larger circle at the end of the line represents this assessment.

Source: Gobble et al., 2016.

Figure I.1: Traditional sequence of instruction and assessment.

Evidence-based instruction focuses on the student's reaction instead of the teacher's delivery, so teachers must direct the lesson while learning is happening and determine the direction to take based on student-produced *evidence*, as figure I.2 (page 8) illustrates. The small dots in figure I.2 represent students, and the big circles represent what the teacher expects students to ultimately know or do (learning target or desired level of proficiency). Notice that students move closer and closer to desired levels of proficiency. They do this by recalling, reflecting on, applying, and reapplying the small components of a given learning target.

Figure I.2: Evidence-based sequence of instruction and assessment.

Think about it this way: figure I.1 is like teaching a child how to ride a bike by making sure he or she knows all the bike parts (pedals, handlebars, and so on) and how they function. Figure I.2 represents how you would actually *teach* a child to ride the bike. You let the child get on the bike right away, and he or she learns to ride while simultaneously making sense of the bike parts.

In evidence-based grading, teachers must remember that instruction has no shape or size. The first step is to realize that lessons are not small, systematic increments to success, but rather *arbitrary reactions* to student input and output. Evidence-based instruction promotes self-reflective interaction with expectations. Subsequently, evidence-based instruction manages and supports a space for learning to occur.

When instruction focuses on reaction, the lesson centers less on the teacher. Students become more involved in their own learning. However, this only happens when teachers use proficiency-based learning targets. *Proficiency-based learning targets* are defined states of competency that act as learning outcomes (Gobble et al., 2016). In *Proficiency-Based Assessment*, Gobble et al. (2016) state that proficiency-based learning targets have three components.

1. **Proficiency language** outlines the intended state of competency. Examples of this language include words such as *effectively*, *main*, *appropriate*, *all*, and *creatively*. These words are important because they contextualize the state of competency for students as well as allow students to accurately perceive their own state of competency. Moreover, these words create the reflective foundation for learners to gain appropriate perspective and prevent them from becoming overconfident in their skills or knowledge.

2. **Measurable language** outlines how students show the extent of their competency. Examples of this language include phrases such as *in writing*, *with sufficient detail*, *in order*, and *with personal connection*. These phrases are important because they state the framework through which we evaluate competency. For example, if the proficiency-based learning target has the measurable language *in writing*, learners know that teachers will evaluate their competency via what they write.

3. **Gradations of competency** are essential for self-reflection and growth. According to Gobble et al. (2016), gradations properly contextualize proficiency, create purpose for instructional activities, make student-produced evidence growth driven, and provide a script for quality feedback. Evidence-based grading is a *method* for learning, not just a way to determine a grade.

Evidence-based instruction means that learning targets are active learning tools for students. Teachers and students use feedback related to the target to help students grow, reflect on learning, organize their thoughts, review work, self-assess, and revise learning to demonstrate growth in a skill area. Clear feedback helps students relate the target to the evidence they create, which is at the center of the learning process. This is similar to backward design, in which the value lies in students knowing expectations for outcomes prior to starting the learning process.

Incorporating reflective and reaction-based instructional practices makes it more likely that students achieve an intended level of mastery. By continuously reflecting and revising, students consistently examine how well they are performing and work to make continuous improvements. This approach asks students to communicate clearly about how they evaluate their learning. Ultimately, by focusing our instruction on reflection and reaction, we give students the structural guidance they need to reach proficiency expectations through proficiency-based targets.

Assessment Gives Students Opportunities for Reflection and Feedback

Asking students to interact reflectively with assessments as often as possible creates a learning environment that fosters continual growth. In evidence-based grading, assessment is a reflective interaction with one's own current state of learning. This essentially means that assessments are events that ask students to assess their own learning regarding *who they are now* and *who they are becoming* in relation to an expectation: the proficiency-based learning target.

For this to happen, students must have the opportunity to distinguish between the *targeted* proficiency level and their *ongoing, developing* performance. Evidence-based grading is based primarily on *quality proficiency-based assessment practices*: "the process of creating, supporting, and monitoring student reflection and thought patterns to achieve an intended state of competency" (Gobble et al., 2016, p. 15).

As evidence-based teachers, we want students to prepare for and summarize their learning reflectively. We want them to be mindful and observant of their progress. In contrast to traditional assessment, evidence-based assessments ask

Interesting ... thought provoking

students to be aware of *how they are producing* the evidence of their learning rather than *what they produce.*

Gobble et al. (2016) refer to this concept as *proficiency-based reflection*—examining one's current state of competency and considering potential next steps to further understanding. These opportunities involve several critical facts.

- Assessments are reflective events.

- Students must be aware of their proficiency level.

- Students must accept feedback.

Assessments Are Reflective Events

If an assessment promotes reflection, efficacy, and self-questioning, then it is more personalized and meaningful for the learner. When teachers approach assessment from the reflection angle, it can guide their instruction and simultaneously provide students with growth feedback tied to clear proficiency-based targets (Chappuis, 2009; Gobble et al., 2016).

Students Must Be Aware of Their Proficiency Level

Proficiency-based reflection helps students become aware of questions that emerge from their interaction with the proficiency-based target. In order for students to answer these questions, we must help them develop proficiency awareness—a personal interpretation of their gradation of competency (Gobble et al., 2016). By being attentive to the state of competency, students not only become more active in their learning but also begin to trust their own self-assessments.

Students Must Accept Feedback

When teachers create assessments that help students reflect and develop proficiency awareness, students more easily understand the relationship between the feedback they receive and their learning. Students will understand that their own learning and development are directly tied to feedback's frequency and quality. And when this happens, students more easily accept even critical feedback.

Teachers should create the following conditions in their classrooms to help students accept and react to feedback (Gobble et al., 2016).

- A learning culture that asks students to make connections, not just produce correct answers

- Events that promote an *active* search for meaning

- A culture focused on growth and development, not fixed ability

- Thinking activities that require collaboration and deliberation

When teachers and students are mindful of the reflection process, they engage in ongoing dialogue about student learning and begin to develop behaviors that promote and encourage improvement.

Teachers Determine Grades With a Calibrated Interpretation of Student Evidence

When *examining the evidence* of a student's work, the teacher decides whether he or she has achieved an expectation. No matter the algorithm or formula, determining proficiency is never as precise as simply reviewing the evidence against expectations. By shifting the grade determination away from mathematical formulas, some teachers continue to think that grading becomes more subjective and less valid. However, evidence-based grading should reduce subjectivity. In an evidence-based model, teachers collaboratively:

- Vet learning targets and gradations of learning

- Create formative assessments

- Review student work to calibrate interpretations

When we make calibrated and common decisions about student evidence to interpret their proficiency, we provide a fair and accurate learning environment superior to one with arbitrary cutoffs or thresholds.

Unlike standards-based grading, which tends to focus on the *quantity* of standards achieved, evidence-based grading focuses on the student's *evidence of proficiency*. In essence, the teacher focuses on the growth within a student's body of work to determine the student's performance. The teacher uses formative assessments to evaluate each student's growth and final grade.

In *Elements of Grading: A Guide to Effective Practice*, Douglas Reeves (2016a) states, "What we ascribe to students must be a matter of judgment as well as the consequence of evidence and reason" (p. 1). Traditional arguments force logical consequence and reason out of the grading conversation and replace them with arguments about accumulating points or other external rewards. Standards-based grading attempts to bring the discussion back to evidence, but it tends to fall short because it relies on the quantity of standards achieved—often appearing more like an achievement checklist than a discussion about learning development.

Evidence-based grading promotes dialogue between teachers and students about how students demonstrate learning and how they actually prove what they know, what they understand, and what they can do. This level of discussion encourages a fundamentally different instructional framework for teaching and learning. In this instructional framework, we must engage students in how they talk about learning, how they demonstrate learning, and how they produce evidence that demonstrates learning. This differs from traditional grading discussions that revolve around points earned, letter grades, or percent averages. Those types of discussions are not about the learning; they are about grades.

In evidence-based grading, the student and teacher discuss the skills achieved and evidence skills were developed. When teacher teams calibrate their expectations, create common assessments to capture evidence of those expectations, and distinguish whether the evidence shows patterns that meet those expectations, we have a process that is more precise than a mathematical formula because we're talking about learning and communicating about growth and gaps.

Schools might struggle in their effort to make changes to grading practices if they continue to focus on standards, topical units, task-based curriculum, rote and short-term memory learning, and mathematical averages. Their conversations can be far more successful with evidence-based grading, which centers on a proficiency-based curriculum, reflective interaction with students, and collaborative and communal discussions about evidence. It is important that the discussions about learning and the evidence of learning remain the focus—be very careful not to fall back into old habits and old arguments about point gathering or worse, grade grubbing.

Five Phases of Implementing Evidence-Based Grading

Schools should not do the work of changing grading practices from the top down. The best chance for making lasting and significant changes in grading practices is through thoughtful and challenging professional development and the creative insights of teachers who are experts in their discipline. Change does not come easily through a sit-and-get, stand-alone professional development day or through a one-size-fits-all model. Instead, professional development must recognize that individual teachers and collaborative teams vary in expertise, knowledge, skill, and perspective. Any school change needs input from these diverse perspectives. This takes time, but when schools implement positive change with thoughtful deliberation and smart intentions, this change can last.

Every teacher brings different strengths and capabilities to work each day. We must value these viewpoints and consider them during the decision-making process. By providing more focused, worthwhile professional experiences for teachers, we can all make sense of best research practices to guide change in our schools.

We rely on long-standing research grounded in the creative process to create individualized, effective professional development experiences. Psychologist and author Mihaly Csikszentmihalyi (1990) presents this process in five interconnected and overlapping stages, which inspired our five-phase process: (1) preparation, (2) incubation, (3) insight, (4) evaluation, and (5) elaboration. Summarizing the creative process based on previous work around the development of change, Csikszentmihalyi (1990) provides a better framework for professional learning among educators.

Many professional learning experiences we have observed tend to be lecture based and noncollaborative. Expert educators collaborate in five very different ways during the decision-making process toward change. As we've found, this allows us to create different forms of professional learning experiences that help us evolve change—by considering what we know, what we think, what we discover, how we evaluate, and why we build change. We believe this is a much more intentional way of approaching change, and we find that it helps us collaborate more effectively among teachers who might have varying thoughts or opinions about what is best for students.

For the purpose of simplicity, this book shows how effective education teams work through these five interconnected phases of the creative process. The phases first appear as separate events, but eventually all phases begin to interact with one another.

Csikszentmihalyi (1990) outlines the five phases of the creative process:

1. **Preparation** is becoming immersed in problematic issues that are interesting and arouse curiosity. *Preparation* is the term that psychologists apply to the first [phase] of the creative process when individuals are starting out and struggling to perfect their craft. Inspiration is what drives the curiosity of both great artists and scientists to persevere through their years of hard work.

2. **Incubation** refers to the period during which ideas churn around below the threshold of consciousness. After an individual has started working on a solution to a problem or has had an idea leading to a novel approach to an effort, the individual enters the incubation stage. According to research psychologists, this stage can last hours, days, months, or years. When individuals try to solve problems consciously, it becomes a linear process, but when problems are left to incubate or simmer, unexpected combinations occur. And it's these unexpected combinations that form domain-changing breakthroughs.

3. **Insight** is the "Aha!" moment when the puzzle starts to come together. The insight stage is also called the *eureka experience*. Some psychologists call it *illumination*. It's the exact moment in time when a problem that an individual has been trying to solve—for days, months, or years—comes together in his or her mind to form a clear resolution. This resolution only emerges after a complex and lengthy process.

4. **Evaluation** occurs when deciding if the insight is valuable and worth pursuing. During the fourth phase of the creative process, individuals must decide if their insights are novel and make sense. In other words, they must analyze the insights to determine if they're truly worth pursuing. If the insight continues to excite and motivate the individual to go forward, then the hard work of turning the creation into a reality begins. Some creativity researchers, such as Harvard University's Teresa M. Amabile (1983), cite motivation as the key factor in the creative process. Regardless of the ingenuity, novelty, or originality of an idea, artwork, or scientific invention, if the creator is unmotivated, the work will never become a reality.

5. **Elaboration** is translating the insight into its final work and constantly nuancing or revising. Throughout the creativity literature, many who have created products that literally changed their domains or disciplines state the necessity of hard work and revision. Yet at the same time, they also state that it doesn't seem like work at all but seems more like play. Additionally, the opinions of others, great awards, and fame mean very little in the end. It's the process of creating that drives them forward toward continuous growth and improvement. (pp. 5–6)

The five phases are crucial to changing mindsets toward an evidence-based grading model—mainly because the change involves not only the way teachers grade students but also the way students and families approach evidence-based grading as part of the learning process of continuous growth. They must be prepared for this shift and understand its purpose and value. Likewise, they will go through a period of wondering if it is working or not—and how. From that point, as we've found, many students and families gain greater insight into how to approach learning as a discussion about skills and not points and percentages or grades.

As we work through this discussion, we strive to share the thinking, debate, and reflections of teacher teams that work to make this shift; likewise, we will share how they engage in important conversations with students and families regarding the shift and its value toward building a clearer, more coherent, and more unified understanding of learning growth.

As you read, consider why each phase fosters greater collaboration between teachers, and how it promotes thoughtful, new conversations with students and families about learning. More specifically, we hope to provide you with a pathway to implementing evidence-based grading—a change we think is significant as schools work to address student growth and learning.

The Structure of This Book

This book outlines one curriculum team's journey to implement evidence-based grading and features a powerful model of professional learning. Team members will navigate challenges, pitfalls, and successes as they engage in each phase of the professional learning process. Along the way, they collaborate, debate ideas, and work to build consensus as they reach toward a new approach to grading grounded in better teaching and learning practices.

In each chapter, we explain a phase, demonstrate change through our team members' points of view, and identify key strategies to support change during the phase. As you'll see, each phase fosters powerful discussions about teaching and student learning.

It's important to note that this is only one way of separating these phases of progression. They are recursive and often overlapping. No one phase is better than another. Professionals always gain insight and go back to prepare, think, or evaluate. Individual educators and teams of educators will move in and among these phases of the creative process—they will revisit, question, react to, and think about them at different times. This allows professionals to reflect, learn, develop new ideas, and build on those ideas.

Chapter 1 examines the preparation phase, comparing evidence-based grading with past grading systems. During this phase, team members are educated about why the shift to evidence-based grading is significant, how and why it is different from past practices, and how it will develop authentic conversations about learning. The team asks questions and begins to grapple with student reflection as a powerful learning experience. Most important, team members will begin to create a shared understanding of what evidence-based grading can do for student achievement in their own subject areas.

Chapters 2 and 3 are about the incubation and insight phases. At these points, the team is really thinking about how to scale learning targets and communicate expectations. The team debates about past grading practices that make sense and question the amount of time the shift might take. The team also wonders about the worth of such a big change, but as insights emerge, the team realizes the value of an evidence-based learning model. Team members are able to see direct relationships between teaching and learning, and they begin to generate collaborative agreements that support student success.

In chapter 4, the team enters the evaluation phase. During this phase, the team examines how well the change is working and critiques its implementation of an evidence-based grading model. Team members evaluate the way students communicate about learning and the clarity and coherence an evidence-based grading model brings to curricular, instructional, and assessment practices. Likewise, they evaluate how well students and parents understand the value of the change—which is equally crucial to its successes. By the end of this journey, the team takes responsibility for further revision and continuous improvement. Through each phase, you will notice team members reflecting on teaching and learning, realizing they need to develop growth-minded students who make learning visible.

Finally, in chapter 5, team members arrive at the elaboration phase with a clear connection between their work and a newfound purpose and a commitment to student learning. With fully developed experiences implementing evidence-based grading, the team works to implement more reflective learning strategies—pushing all students to greater levels of achievement. The team members also emphasize effective feedback and instruction that create a perpetually dynamic learning process. The team embraces change through more accurate reflection practices, revisions to instruction, and instruction-aligned assessment. Ultimately, the team's patterns of teaching merge to unify its shared curriculum, instruction, and assessment into a singular process with a mindset for continuous improvement.

Taking the time to work through these phases of professional development sustains a culture of innovation and continuous improvement—an engaging collaborative discussion where curriculum, instruction, and assessment work together as one. After you implement evidence-based grading practices, we are confident that you will create smarter conversations about teaching and learning that will have lasting effects on students.

Chapter 1

Preparation

A shift to evidence-based grading is the logical next step for teams that are committed to the work of proficiency-based assessment. Evidence-based grading and proficiency-based assessment work hand in hand. An evidence-based grading model supports the type of discussion and dialogue that proficiency-based assessments enable. In fact, we feel that the shift to evidence-based grading is the natural outgrowth of proficiency-based assessment. However, as we know from experience, a shift to evidence-based grading is a very different challenge for a school to manage, as it upends decades of how we've traditionally communicated about student abilities. Likewise, a shift to evidence-based grading demands that all stakeholders in students' education are clear on this grading model's value and understand its purpose. This demand requires clarity and preparation.

As we consider working with schools and teams that plan to move toward an evidence-based grading model, we recognize that this change confronts past grading practices and undoes many routine approaches to teaching and learning. Likewise, preparing to change to an evidence-based grading model requires preparing all who are connected to the change—teachers, students, and guardians and parents. All these stakeholders must understand the value of this change and how it can foster better discussions around teaching and learning.

This chapter walks our team through the preparation phase.

- How teachers begin to think differently about their own instructional practices
- How students begin to talk differently about their own learning

- How parents or guardians can better understand education in a way that nurtures lifelong learning, understanding grading as a process of learning growth rather than a strict statement of measured ability

At our school, we ask ourselves, "How do we build from the good work we are already doing and make it better? What should we consider next?" In a culture of continuous improvement, teachers and students are always looking to improve on their current practices and find new and improved ways to support learning. Evidence-based grading and the conversations that are required for successful implementation fit well within a culture of continuous improvement. It encourages learning as an ongoing discussion of growth and development. Surprisingly, this is an unfamiliar mindset to students and families, who are used to grades that denote success or failure. These generations of students have been comfortable with a system of grading based on accumulating points and averages that somehow reflect intelligence. Shifting away from this long-standing mindset challenges us because it changes the way we communicate about learning.

Although school leaders may work diligently to prepare for professional development, we often hear from those for whom professional learning has become a stand-alone event with little follow-through. We designed this chapter to examine and suggest ways to first prepare faculty for a change in grading practices and how to then implement the change effectively. For this book's purpose, we focus our attention on actually implementing an evidence-based grading model as the team grapples with its own questions and challenges.

Following are three key points to remember during the preparation phase.

1. To develop shared commitments, the collaborative team must be willing to question and challenge its current grading practices and then agree on more effective strategies that implement an evidence-based approach.

2. For equity, the team must be able to develop consensus and inter-rater reliability around grading practices. Inter-rater reliability simply means the team is calibrated around how it actually assesses the evidence of student proficiency—what represents proficiency to one teacher should represent proficiency to all teachers on the team.

3. For clarity and communication, team members must fully understand *why* they are being asked to consider changing their traditional grading practices and be able to explain this change clearly to both students and their parents.

Preparing individuals for change in grading practices goes beyond strong communication strategies. In many schools, every teacher might have his or her own grading policy and procedures; there might be multiple grading scales; and students might be graded differently depending on their teachers, not the subjects. These inconsistencies lead to inequitable grading practices. Hurdling traditional practices that sustain inequities and inconsistencies is one challenge evidence-based grading works to overcome. This shift means that a team must build a shared understanding and a shared commitment to change where consistent evaluation is valued.

As you read about our team's journey of moving to an evidence-based grading model, consider the ways the team prepares for change—learning, investigating, questioning, and fleshing out each member's knowledge and understanding. Also, think about how the team considers implementing the change and makes the decisions to bring about this shift toward greater consistency and equity.

We created this team scenario with some of our best teachers in mind—some willing to change, some questioning change, and some holding back. Each teacher is a change agent. What does each change agent need? How do leaders support teachers' efforts early in the change process? How does an organization create and sustain meaningful change? As you read our team's story, ask yourself how the team answers the following challenges.

- Is every team member fully committed to the value of evidence-based grading, and is he or she clear on how to talk about its purpose and intention so students and parents clearly understand the change in grading practices?

- Is the team paying close attention to inter-rater reliability in its grading practices? Is each member implementing a shared and communicated agreement about what it means to meet or exceed the team's stated learning targets?

- Is the team identifying ways in which a shift to evidence-based grading fosters better communication about teaching and learning practices?

Our Team's Story

Toward the end of May, Mario and his team are considering their next action steps. The team has worked hard for the past year to implement best practices of proficiency-based assessment. Members see success in their approach to curriculum, instruction, and assessment. Moreover, they are getting students to discuss learning and learning targets more often, rather than fighting to earn points. Seeing this stride forward, they know their next step requires a different approach to grades and feedback. This year, Mario, Joni, Maya, Britney, and Kevin are positioned and determined to implement an evidence-based grading model as a natural extension of their proficiency-based assessment practices.

Mario, the team leader, has spent a lot of time grappling with evidence-based grading's concepts, and he is eager to work with the team and lead discussions around its implementation. Maya is in her second year of teaching and feels more comfortable with the curriculum than she did at first. Britney is in her seventh year of teaching and is indifferent to adopting a new grading system. Based on past experiences, Joni and Kevin know that a change to evidence-based grading means breaking away from years of past practices. Joni also notes that the shift isn't just going to be hard for teachers to fully understand—it is going to be difficult for students as well. Likewise, it will confuse parents who have only ever known a points-and-percentage-based grading system.

Luckily, a couple of the content-based curriculum teams in the school have already made the shift to evidence-based grading, so our team thinks it can gather some good advice from other faculty members about how they already implemented and communicated the change to evidence-based grading. By no means does anyone claim to be an expert on the topic, but the teams that implemented the new model really like the outcome: discussing learning with students instead of confronting them about points and percentages.

Mario is excited but anxious, as team members are going to implement evidence-based grading into their subject area in a few months. At the end of May, the team gathers in a classroom to discuss its approach to implementation. John, director of assessment, and Kaori, assistant superintendent of curriculum, lead the meeting. These two school leaders worked previously with a number of teams through the challenging shift. John and Kaori welcome the team and begin to discuss evidence-based grading. They are up-front about the need to shift away from past grading practices and recognize the effort it will take. The teams that have implemented evidence-based grading continue to encourage them to move forward with the change.

"As other teachers are saying," notes John, "once you shift to evidence-based grading, you will never want to go back."

John and Kaori help Mario's team by introducing a clear protocol to follow during evidence-based grading implementation. The first step is to ensure the team has a clear understanding of the purpose of making this change.

Kaori begins the meeting with two questions: "Why are we moving to an evidence-based grading system anyway? What benefit does evidence-based grading have that our traditional grading practices lack?"

The team sits silently, and Kaori, not expecting an answer, continues, "It's important to start with understanding *why* we are making this change. Our mission is to ensure the most accurate and clear communication about learning to promote success for *all* students. Evidence-based grading principles support this mission."

John then takes his turn. "It's frustrating, but our current system, which we've been using for decades, doesn't support our mission of clear communication. This came to me when I thought about real-life student experiences with grading and reporting practices. Let's start with a scenario. Let's suppose a student gets the following grades on five exams for one six-week grading period: 40, 60, 80, 90, 90. What grade does the student deserve?"

Mario replies, "I know this is not the answer we will give by the end of this meeting, but I would say 72 percent based on the way we calculate grades now."

"Well," John says, "a few things come to mind when I hear that. First, the student's last two assessments yielded a score of 90, and also the student never scored in the 70s at any point during these assessments. If we look through the student's grades, it appears that over time, he made significant improvements. The student learned *over time*. If we calculate the student's grade average, aren't we really discounting his growth? Aren't we assigning a grade for the student based on what he wasn't able to prove instead of what he is *now* able to prove?"

Maya speaks up. "I agree, but the student also has to be accountable for past mistakes. Averaging all those grades together is more accurate because the student was only at 90 percent for a short time period out of all the assessments. Therefore, a 72.5 percent, or C grade, is really a good picture of the student during the course. He didn't do well the whole time, just part of the time."

John says, "That may be so, but think of it this way. Do you remember learning how to ride a bike? When you learned, did you factor in all the times you fell to determine whether you could ride, or did you just finally learn to ride? You didn't just average your ability to ride the bike and say, 'I ride a bike at 72 percent.'"

Team members nod in agreement. John continues, "Would you consider a student who can now fluently speak another language not fluent because she made many mistakes along the way? Of course not. Or how about a student who didn't know algebra or chemistry at the beginning of the school year but learned it by the end?"

John moves to make his point. "All learning is based on growth. In fact, that is the definition of learning. Evidence-based grading is a growth-based learning model and supports the expression of skill acquisition and knowledge. Our current system of grading does not express anything but percentages or point earnings. It doesn't communicate learning's growth and development.

"Let's consider another example. Suppose a student gets the following scores: 0, 0, 0, 100, 100, 100. What percentage will she receive?"

Kevin says, "Traditionally, the student would get a 50 percent. She would fail the class."

"Correct," John replies. "Now, how many 100 percent grades would the student need to get in order to offset all those zeros and earn an A?"

The group is slow to answer this time. Some members mumble a few answers, but nothing seems correct. John explains, "In order to get an A grade, the student would need twenty-seven more 100 percent grades in the gradebook to offset the initial three zeros. In other words, it is almost impossible to outpace a particularly low grade, especially a zero."

"So, you are saying we shouldn't use zeros. I get it. But what about the student who just doesn't do the work?" asks Maya.

Kaori says, "Behavior and academics must not coexist in one single letter grade. The comingling of behavior, skills, attendance, attitude, work ethic, and skills performance creates lack of clarity about why the student gets a certain grade. We then assume a lot about what is behind the grade. Think of the letter grade *B*. Some parents may think it means *smart but the class is hard*, while other parents may think *not as smart as other students in the class*. Some may think that their child didn't work hard enough. Too many assumptions cause the grade to be less accurate. Therefore, it is not aligned with our mission, which is ensuring the most accurate assessment and communication of student growth and performance."

John says, "We see this same problem in the assessments themselves. Let's assume you have an exam this week. One student skips the test and another gets all the questions wrong . . . yet they both get a zero in the gradebook. So, what does that zero represent? Does it represent a lack of effort or a lack of knowledge? You really don't know the grade's intent on a report card."

The team acknowledges his point. John continues, "So, can we agree now that zeros are not effective, averages do not work, and grade information must be reported separately from behavior as a way to communicate meaningfully?"

The team understands exactly what John is saying, and each member thinks about how the years of past grading practices might not have been equitable to students.

Kaori starts the next segment. "In evidence-based grading, we assess students on a gradation of learning that has four levels. Why only four levels? Let me explain. It is essential as assessors that we possess the capability to articulate a clear description of each level of achievement as well as the differences between these levels. This clarity about each level of achievement is not only important for equitable and just assessment of student performance, it is also important for feedback, curriculum, and instruction. In fact, evidence-based systems are based on this gradation of achievement and the ability to articulate it. Without clarity, it is impossible to assess students accurately.

"There are four levels in our system," Kaori continues. "Fewer levels means that students are classified more accurately. As Thomas R. Guskey points out on page 36 of his 2015 book *On Your Mark*, 'essentially, as the number of grade categories goes up, the chance of two equally competent judges assigning exactly the same grade to the same sample of a student's work diminishes significantly.' Let's do a little exercise."

"We currently use a one-hundred-point scale," John says. "Together as a group, think about an assignment you recently gave to your students."

Joni says, "A free-response writing assignment about the Battle of the Bulge."

"Great!" says John. "Now think about the students' grades, and ponder this question: What is the difference between a student who gets an 85 percent and a student who gets an 86 percent? Keep in mind that in order to have an accurate and fair grading system, the assessor must be able to articulate the difference between these two percentages."

The team is silent for a few seconds, and then Mario laughs. "I can't," he says. "There is no real difference between 85 percent and 86 percent." The others agree.

"The more levels we have," John says, "the more we run the risk of potentially giving an incorrect rating. Even worse, we give inaccurate feedback. This is why we must have the fewest achievement levels possible that still promote quality feedback. This is why we use four."

Kaori says, "Evidence-based grading is based on achieving a level of proficiency—proficiency in a skill or proficiency in consolidating information into actionable thoughts. This proficiency is assessed by a gradation of achievement that represents an assessor's expectations. Expectations have gradations, and you use them to evaluate the current evidence of performance. Does that make sense?"

Again, team members nod, and Kaori continues, "Therefore, we must attach levels to our expectations. We believe that there are only four levels of an expectation, nothing more. There is no such thing as a 'super-duper' expectation or 'terribly, horribly not-even-close' standards. Or, at least there shouldn't be."

"What about our A, B, C system? That is a five-level system, and we have been using that for years," Maya points out.

"Yes, that's true," John says, "but what is the difference between a D and an F? Does a D student know a little bit more than an F student? Do schools not worry about students with D grades? When a student is doing D work, don't we work to provide him or her with interventions?"

"So, is a 4 really just an A in this system?" Mario asks with a bit of confusion.

"That's a good question," Kaori says. "I believe a lot of teachers might think the same way—that evidence-based grading substitutes numbers for letters. It is hard to think this way, but the numbers 4, 3, 2, and 1 have no numerical value; they are just positional markers that communicate the location one occupies relative to an expectation. You could use checks, pluses, animals, or letter combinations . . . it doesn't matter. The preponderance of evidence is what matters in the evidence-based model, not numbers and scaled ranges of accumulated points. The 4 simply represents that a student is past the expected performance level, a 3 means the student is at the expected performance level, a 2 indicates he or she is approaching the expected performance level, and a 1 indicates that the student isn't even close."

Shaking her head, Britney asks, "Why isn't 4 the expectation? Isn't that what you want a student to ultimately achieve?"

John says, "For an evidence-based model, the expectation must never be the top rung of the ladder, so to speak. There is always space to go beyond the expectation. Expectations need levels to have context, and the expected level must sit at the third rung."

Still not convinced, Joni says, "By this logic, a B is the expectation in our current system, but we don't think that way. Students want an A. The A is the expectation, but there is nothing past an A."

John says, "An A+ is past an A." He pauses as he writes out the current A, B, C, D, F model's plus/minus scale and then says, "If A is the expectation, A+ is the above and beyond. Then it would be all B and C, and then D and F."

The team understands that this is a societal shift in thinking, not only an educational shift.

Kaori says, "In an evidence-based model, we judge students against a criterion, meaning if they show competency in certain criteria, we deem them competent. They would get the A, or the 3, or the checkmark, and so on. If they earn it, they deserve it. Actually, we have seen very little difference between evidence-based courses and non-evidence-based courses regarding grade distribution. In fact, they are almost identical, with the exception that in evidence-based courses, there are almost no failures. And this is what we want! Success for every student!"

Britney asks, "OK, I get all this, but if we can't use points, what do we use to grade? I can't seem to picture how we grade without points. Do I just give students a 4, 3, 2, or 1 on everything but use a letter grade for assignments in the gradebook?"

Having heard this question before, John says, "Gradebooks are set up with learning targets, not assignments or assessments. You are simply inserting a target and a number for the proficiency a student has demonstrated on that target."

The group still seems confused, so Kaori begins writing the following on the board. "In our gradebooks now, we see this."

- Assignment: Score

- Assignment: Score

- Assessment: Score

- Assignment: Score

- Assessment: Score

"So it looks like the following." She continues writing.

- Homework 1: 10/12

- Formative worksheet: 10/10

- Quiz: 23/30

- Project: 36/40

- Test: 44/50

"However, in evidence-based grading, we see the following." She writes on the board.

- Target: Proficiency score

- Target: Proficiency score

- Target: Proficiency score

"So, it would look like this." She finishes writing on the board.

- I can explain . . . 4

- I can create . . . 3

- I can identify . . . 3

Kevin, looking a bit confused, asks, "What happens to all the assignments? We don't report them?"

"In an evidence-based system, reporting focuses on acquiring proficiency, not achieving a task. So, accumulating tasks is not necessary to report, just the most prominent or current state of proficiency."

"So, I just replace the score based on the evidence I have to interpret?" Kevin asks.

"Yes!" Kaori says. "When you convert to evidence-based grading, your grading policy becomes the professional interpretation of evidence, nothing more. This is Guskey's principle, and we feel it is the fairest and most accurate way to determine student grades."

The team members like the grading policy's simplicity, but they feel nervous about the policy's subjectivity.

"When teams collaboratively vet expected evidence from student performance," John explains, "they also are collaboratively vetting their expectations. This clarifies feedback and instruction for students. In terms of assessment, the curriculum team has deeply calibrated and scrutinized student performance so it is far less subjective than a non-evidence-based grading system."

"When a team attempts to do all this outside of an evidence-focused grading system," Kaori says, "teams must write the exam together. That's easy, but how do they decide how many questions to put on the exam? How do they decide how many points each question is worth, and how those points relate mathematically to total points for the semester or term? How do they decide how to reward answers with points? How do they decide how to award those points as they observe performance nuances? What assumptions can the team make about borderline answers or performances? All these layers are at play in non-evidence-based grading courses."

"More important," John says, "as you begin your journey, we need to ensure that we calibrate all perspectives, use high-quality assessments, and give all parties the right evidence. In this way, we make feedback purposeful and useful. We work to create these elements when implementing evidence-based grading.

"Remember, we are moving to this model for two reasons: First, the traditional grading model exposes students to a false sense of mastery because it has teachers approve students' short-term acquisition of knowledge as learning. Second, and even worse, students are not developing the skills to identify and articulate their current state of learning. We feel evidence-based grading successfully addresses both concerns."

Kaori asks the next logical question in order to move the team to its next phase of learning: "Can anyone tell me what a good learning target looks like?"

Team members spend the rest of the meeting discussing the next steps toward implementation and set an implementation date for the new process. The team knows summer is a good time to rest before the challenge of implementing its new grading model.

The Four Commitments in Evidence-Based Grading

In the preparation phase of team learning, members must commit to certain practices and perspectives. They must first resolve central issues and achieve coherence and clarity in order to build a solid foundation from which to learn. Committing to these perspectives is the first step to implementing evidence-based grading. Before team members can move forward, they must come to a consensus on the following four commitments of evidence-based grading.

1. Agree that the percentage system is a flawed grading model.

2. Eliminate four specific grading errors.

3. Focus on grading proficiency.

4. Use student-produced evidence.

Agree That the Percentage System Is a Flawed Grading Model

One of the more interesting questions we get when talking to colleagues about grading is, Where did the current grading system come from anyway? That is an interesting story.

It all began in the 19th century. Those few students who were lucky enough to forgo the farm and go to school typically went to a small, one-room schoolhouse with a teacher who usually taught the same students for many years. The teacher would deliver oral feedback on student performance a few times a year during home visits with students and their parents. Similarly, in the first half of the 19th century, most colleges and universities provided students with feedback in writing driven mostly by descriptive adjectives (Durm, 1993).

At the college and university level, grading was a hodgepodge of systems as schools experimented with various models. It wasn't until the late 19th century that some major universities assembled what became the 21st century grading system's foundation (Durm, 1993). For example, the 1877 Harvard University faculty records show students were ranked on merit in six divisions, with Division I representing 90 or more on a scale to 100. Division II was 89–75, Division III was 74–60, Division IV was 59–50, Division V was 49–40, and Division VI was below 40. Later, in 1886, Harvard faculty records show an updated reporting model that sorted students by who scored in the 90s, 80s, and 70s. Class IV included students who passed but did so without distinction. Class V included students who did not pass the term (Durm, 1993).

In 1897, the Mount Holyoke College faculty adapted the Harvard model and developed a marking system that most resembles what 21st century schools use.

A: Excellent (95–100 percent)

B: Good (85–94 percent)

C: Fair (76–84 percent)

D: Pass (75 percent)

E: Fail (below 75 percent; Durm, 1993)

In the early 20th century, many colleges added a point scale that designated 4.0 for an A, 3.0 for a B, 2.0 for a C, and 1.0 for a D (Durm, 1993). What we find most interesting in this brief history is that what was once a classification system used at the college and university level has morphed into a method for determining K–12 student grades.

As the number of students in schools began to surge in the late 19th and early 20th centuries, school systems had to determine a more efficient model for grouping students within larger schools. The most logical model—though not necessarily the most educationally sound one—involved grouping students by age and placing them in different grade levels. For example, schools placed five-year-olds in kindergarten classrooms, six-year-olds in first-grade classrooms, seven-year-olds in second-grade classrooms, and so on.

As the number of students in schools grew, it became difficult for teachers to do home visits to share feedback and student progress with parents. Teachers in elementary schools began writing narrative descriptions of how students were performing in class. They developed report cards to provide students and their families with more formal evaluations of which skills and content students had mastered and which required improvement (Guskey & Bailey, 2001). In truth, schools planted the seeds for evidence-based grading in early 20th century elementary schools.

As the number of students enrolling in middle and high schools grew exponentially in the early 20th century and specific subject-matter instruction became more prevalent, teachers needed a more efficient method for grading student progress. Teachers looked to colleges and universities for that method and found a percentage model used for students who were just a few years older. As more schools and teachers began looking to colleges for a grading model to use in public middle and high schools, they cemented the percentage system as a grading practice that we continue to use in the 21st century—more than 120 years later. In looking back over those 120 years in education, we see an efficient, yet misguided and ineffective grading system.

Even a casual observer must be willing to admit that concretizing percentages doesn't make a lot of sense. Is 50 percent always failure? What if a professional baseball player hits a single 50 percent of the time he is at bat? We would not consider that a failure. In fact, this player wouldn't just be admitted to the U.S. National Baseball Hall of Fame; Major League Baseball would probably rename the Hall of Fame after him! Conversely, what if a doctor who performs surgery ten times a week had a 90 percent survival rate? In other words, one out of ten times, the patient dies on the table. Would we really consider this 90 percent success rate excellent? Would we give this doctor an A? More important, would we recruit this doctor for our next surgery? No!

Common sense suggests that as a profession, we have known for more than a century that the percentage system is a flawed grading model that simply has to go. We cannot continue to perpetuate a system that is unfair, is inaccurate, and lacks meaningful feedback to students.

Eliminate Four Specific Grading Errors

One of the more instructive books for leaders is *Good to Great: Why Some Companies Make the Leap . . . and Others Don't* by Jim Collins (2001). With his research team, Collins studies how organizations transition from average performance relative to their peers to outstanding and unparalleled performance. Describing one of his more interesting findings, Collins (2001) suggests that:

> Most of us . . . have ever expanding "to do" lists, trying to build momentum by doing, doing, doing—and doing more. And it rarely works. Those who built the good-to-great companies, however, made as much use of "stop doing" lists as the "to do" lists. They displayed a remarkable discipline to unplug all sorts of extraneous junk. (p. 139)

In our own district, we have used the idea of the *stop doing* list. We use it as a tool to determine the extent to which our practices and procedures support our mission of success for every student, and to inform our fundamental purpose around student learning. When we turned the spotlight on the grading practices in our own school, we found that there were a number of practices we had to stop doing immediately. There are many past grading practices we call *traps*—practices that work against our core beliefs around continuous growth, learning, and success for every student.

In *FAST Grading: A Guide to Implementing Best Practices*, Douglas Reeves (2016b) identifies three grading practices he believes are inconsistent with the idea that grades should be fair, accurate, and effective. Reeves (2016b) argues that we must stop using zeros, averages, and grades as rewards. We agree wholeheartedly. After exploring grading practices in our own district, we found two more grading practices to add to the *stop doing* list.

1. Stop using grades as punishment (or as rewards, as Reeves [2016b] notes).

2. Stop weighting grades.

As we worked with curriculum teams in our own district and districts across North America, we formulated the following *stop doing* list for those teachers and teams interested in challenging the traditional grading model. The following are four grading traps that affect students in unexpected and significant ways.

1. Zeros

2. Averages

3. Grades as rewards or punishment

4. Weighted grades

Zeros

Using zeros seems to be one of the most ingrained grading practices in many U.S. districts and schools. Unfortunately, from the student's perspective, teachers wield the zero grade as a weapon rather than an accurate reflection of what the student knows or is able to do. While there are many issues with the zero, especially in conjunction with the percentage system and averaging (described in the next section), our issues with the zero are focused more on the fact that it rarely, if ever, accurately measures student learning and achievement.

Grades should represent what students know and are able to do related to the standards, objectives, and learning targets of their course or grade level. We need to separate achievement and behavior grades. When we provide students with feedback, we must be willing to include both their academic achievement and their academic behaviors, including attendance, organizational skills, time management, academic integrity, classroom communication skills, and so on. A more troubling aspect of current grading models is that grades don't just evaluate academic skills; they evaluate behaviors as well. As educators, we tend to throw all feedback into the mix, kind of like a grading "stew." In the end, we aren't even sure what we actually graded.

When we ask educators why they feel the zero is an effective grading tool, we hear a variation on the same theme: "When students see the zero in the gradebook, it motivates them to get their work done." We are not convinced. While there may be a few students who are actually motivated to do better when they see a zero grade, we hear just the opposite when we talk to students about their grades and grading practices. In our experience, we hear and see students get frustrated once they see the zero or zeros in the gradebook. They often feel that the teacher has given up on them, so they are far less likely to put in extra effort in class.

Additionally, though we have searched far and wide, we simply have not uncovered any education research that demonstrates the positive effect of the zero grade on student motivation and learning.

Our biggest problem with the zero, however, has less to do with the student and more to do with us as professional educators. We doubt that very few if any teachers enter the profession looking forward to using grades as weapons and dropping zeros into the gradebook as an instructive tool. While teachers often give zeros as punishment, we also know that most teachers do not enjoy giving zeros and do so with regret and frustration that the student is not completing his or her work or meeting academic expectations. That said, when we give the zero grade to a student for failing to complete work, we are not teaching him or her responsibility at all; we are, instead, abdicating our own responsibility to the process of teaching and learning.

Averages

In *The Flaw of Averages: Why We Underestimate Risk in the Face of Uncertainty*, Sam L. Savage (2012) makes a compelling case for ignoring the tendency to rely on averages as a measure of central tendency. His groundbreaking research at Stanford University demonstrates how using averages contributed to inaccurate weather predictions, failed business models, and the 2000s' housing bubble. When we examine the use of averages in grading, we see the same problems. Let's consider the following example of Jamie, a member of Ms. Ortiz's seventh-grade science class.

At the beginning of the year, Jamie fails to turn in the three homework assignments that Ms. Ortiz distributes in the first two weeks of class. So, to start the school year, Jamie has three zeros in the gradebook. Then, let's presume Jamie somehow finds these zeros not at all demoralizing but instead motivating. Jamie completes the next three homework assignments and, remarkably, scores 100 percent on each. The gradebook then looks like figure 1.1.

Student	Homework 1	Homework 2	Homework 3	Homework 4	Homework 5	Homework 6
Jamie	0	0	0	100	100	100

Figure 1.1: Jamie's homework scores.

It doesn't take a degree in applied mathematics to determine that the average grade for this student is still 50 percent—an F. In fact, even more disturbing is, once the teacher records the three zeros and three one hundred scores in the gradebook, it will take nine 100 percent grades for Jamie to earn a C or 70 percent, and twenty-seven *more* 100 percent grades for Jamie to earn an A.

Ken O'Connor (2009) summarizes this point perfectly in his book *How to Grade for Learning, K–12*: the major concern with averaging is that "outlier scores" have a huge impact on rating. O'Connor (2009) states that averaging "overemphasizes outlier scores [in final student rating], which are more often low outliers" (p. 90).

But what happens when we use the average to determine a student's grade, and we remove the extreme outliers? What is the negative effect of averaging on a typical student's grade? Let's consider the following example of Anna, who is in Mr. Tripp's ninth-grade algebra class. Although mathematics does not come easily to Anna, she works very hard and is determined to do well. She starts out slowly but improves throughout the semester.

In the first semester, Anna feels good about her progress and her level of achievement in algebra. She knows that she worked hard and that her hard work paid off in the end. She feels that she definitely understands the material, and she is confident about moving to the next semester—until, that is, Anna gets a harsh lesson in the use of averages in grading. When Anna sees her final grade for the first semester, it looks like figure 1.2.

Student	Test 1	Test 2	Test 3	Test 4	Test 5	Semester Grade
Anna	40	60	80	90	90	72 percent

Figure 1.2: Anna's test scores.

Anna is devastated. She felt good about her hard work and resulting improvement. However, once Mr. Tripp averaged her grades together, it came out to a 72 percent, or a C–. The next semester does not go as well for Anna. Her frustration with her first semester's performance causes her to lose motivation, and she doesn't work as hard.

Anna's example is actually a true story and a perfect illustration of the absurdity of averaging grades over time. Not only does the C– grade not reflect Anna's level of *achievement* or *improvement* at the end of the term, but at no point during the term did Anna ever score in the C range!

You may wonder if we would feel as strongly if we were to invert Anna's grades, beginning the term with 90s and ending up with a 40. Of course, we would! In no way does the grade of C– tell us the story of her achievement. If Anna is achieving low marks at the end of the semester, she should receive a failing grade. The point remains the same: using averages in grading simply does not give an accurate and complete picture of student learning and achievement.

Grades as Rewards or Punishment

Ensuring that grading is an accurate, fair, and meaningful experience for both teachers and students is complicated. We find that in a significant number of cases, grades are based in part on student behavior. Generally speaking, teachers give well-behaved students bonuses or extra credit, and reduce the grades of students who misbehave. In *A Repair Kit for Grading: 15 Fixes for Broken Grades* (Second Edition), Ken O'Connor (2011) puts it this way:

> We know that the grading practices of some teachers have contributed to grade inflation for some students by including desired behaviors unrelated to achievement, while other students who achieve at a high level have received deflated grades because of their failure to exhibit these same behaviors. (p. 19)

The assumption behind this practice is that students are motivated to behave properly through the positive or negative reinforcement of the grades they receive for behavior. The grades become the stick for keeping students in line.

There are, of course, two problems with this grading practice. First, it doesn't always work. Not all students are motivated to behave well out of fear of the resulting grade. Some students are naturally well behaved and do not need the extrinsic motivation to continue to be so, while other students simply do not care that their misbehavior somehow translates into a low grade.

Second, grading based on behavior makes it difficult for students, parents, and teachers to determine whether a student actually understands the intended standards and objectives for the material. Does the grade represent achievement of a learning outcome when a teacher adds or subtracts points for behavior?

Students should be able to identify their understanding of each standard in a course and how their performances on various assignments combine to create a final grade. When behavior is included in this mix, teachers cannot effectively describe to students how to improve. For some students, a C grade means they do not understand the material; for others, a C means they did not complete their assignments; for still others, a C means they did not participate as the teacher expected. There is no way to know the root cause of the grade.

Weighted Grades

Weighting grades clouds and distorts how we communicate about learning growth. When teachers weight grades, they add another level of confusion to the evaluation process, to a student's understanding of feedback, and to what is and isn't valued in the learning process. As we launched into the grading initiative in our own district, we focused particularly on the negative effects of using zeros and averages. As we began talking with teachers, we found that while zeros and averages were ubiquitous, other factors also had inadvertent effects on student grades, namely how teachers weight grades.

Weighting grades communicates that not all assignments and assessments are created equal. In a traditional grading system, each assessment is worth a specific number of points. This number of points represents the assessment's *weight*; more points means a bigger impact on the overall grade. As a teacher creates an assessment, he or she indicates that assessment's importance through the total number of points assigned.

Most teachers are very purposeful with weighting each assessment, assigning the most points to the most important or acceptable work. Many teachers are unaware of these weighting choices' ultimate effect on a final grade. The result is utter confusion. An evidence-based grading model works toward a greater level of simplicity and clarity around teaching and learning by focusing on a description of the expected learning skills.

At a teacher meeting, we worked to clarify why weighted grades are so problematic. We provided teachers with a set of assignments and grades for one student. The set included ten homework assignments, three quizzes, and two tests. Percent correct indicated the student's performance on the assignments. We asked each teacher to develop a final grade for the student using his or her current grading system to assign points and weights to each type of assignment. The group was shocked to learn the range of grades that resulted from these individual systems. The same student, with the same scores on the same assignments, received grades from A to D, depending on the teacher's weighting system. Some teachers favored homework grades, while others placed more emphasis on tests. Each choice provided a different weight and, thus, a different final grade.

This is not the only way weighting plays out in a final grade. Inside each assessment is a number of questions or tasks, and each question is also assigned weight by how many points it is worth. This internal weighting can have unintended consequences on a student's final grade.

Consider the following grading scenario. Mr. Pham assigns an essay question worth ten points on a chapter test worth a total of fifty points. He scales all tests to be worth one hundred points and enters the percent correct in the gradebook. That one essay question is worth twenty points in the gradebook. At the end of the six-week term, Mr. Pham has assigned a total of four hundred points' worth of material. That one essay question is now worth 5 percent of a student's final grade! This might have been a very meaningful essay question, but it is difficult to argue that one essay question on one test given on one day can adequately demonstrate 5 percent of a student's learning in a course. Figure 1.3 shows an example of a weighted gradebook.

		Weight	Tests	Percentage of Grade	Homework	Percentage of Grade	Participation	Percentage of Grade
Category Weights			A		B		C	
A	Tests	40	10	2.6	15	15.0	100	20.0
B	Homework	40	56	14.5	10	10.0		
C	Participation	20	10	2.6	10	10.0		
D			10	2.6	5	5.0		
E			40	10.4				
F			15	3.9				
			6	1.6				
			7	1.8				
Total Points in a Category			154	40.0	40	40.0	100	20

Figure 1.3: Weighted gradebook example.

Weighting within a grading system requires students to play a different grading game for each class. These differences in grading can lead to confusion and frustration. Students must ask themselves, "Is this a teacher who values homework? Should I only worry about the tests? What is the most important question on the assessment?"

A grading system should allow students to focus on where they are in their learning journey with respect to the learning targets.

Focus on Grading Proficiency

In our estimation, education and assessment's goal is to report grades that are accurate, consistent, meaningful, and supportive of learning. We can never realize this mission if teachers are not *empirical* about their approach to interpreting student performance. This means that teachers must directly experience and interpret each student's performance *through the evidence of proficiency* that an assessment process produces.

The dictionary defines *evidence* as "something that furnishes proof" (Evidence, n.d.). The benefit of basing grading on evidence is that it provides the teacher, student, and parents with proof that the student has learned. When we collect evidence with fidelity, it presents the most accurate picture of the student's learning—not points, numbers, or any other mathematical metric.

When evidence is at the center of grading practices, teachers can embrace the inherent nuance and context in teaching and learning instead of fearing them. Focusing on evidence reminds us that learning is a process that takes place over time. Collecting each piece of evidence at the logical time provides feedback to the student about who he or she is now as a learner in conjunction with future opportunities to show mastery and continuous growth.

Teachers must commit to the idea of *proficiency* to successfully use evidence in grading practices. Proficiency is the measure of a student's mastery of the essential standards or targets for a course—in other words, how well a student applies the essential learning of the course. Teachers must base grades on proficiency levels rather than on points earned, thus making it easier to identify areas of strength and address areas of concern for each student. This helps ensure that a student's final grade represents his or her *competency* in a course's learning expectations.

Moreover, while traditional points-based grading systems attempt to fuse feedback, achievement results, behavior, and performance expectations into a single percentage, a proficiency-based grading model separately communicates the following about a student.

- Learning goals or targets
- Level of proficiency in each learning target
- Progress toward proficiency in each learning target
- Areas of success and growth

Learning Goals or Targets

Focusing on proficiency in grading promotes the clear and articulated use of specific learning goals or targets, the differentiated instruction that accompanies those targets, and the logical interventions that result from their accurate assessment. Teachers who use learning targets in grading are more inclined to ask themselves, "What evidence of proficiency are we looking for in this course or content area? How well do students receive my instruction? Do students know whether they are competent in a skill?" Figure 1.4 shows an example of a proficiency-based learning target for using maps.

4	3	2	1
Use maps of different scales to describe the locations of different cultural and environmental characteristics.	Use maps of different scales to describe the locations of similar cultural and environmental characteristics.	Use maps of the same scale to describe the locations of similar cultural and environmental characteristics.	Use a map to describe the locations of similar cultural and environmental characteristics.

Figure 1.4: Proficiency-based learning target example.

Level of Proficiency in Each Learning Target

Teachers often include corollary information about learning targets in their grading practices and use mathematical averaging to determine the final proficiency score. We suggest that this is an incomplete practice. Since proficiency-based learning targets are the organizational structure of evidence-based grading, the results are based on the student's proficiency level in each target.

While many teachers have used this practice before, they often overlook a key question when doing so: Does this student produce *enough* evidence in a particular learning target to determine proficiency? Teachers must use proficiency-level gradation, along with common formative assessments, to arrive at a student's proficiency score but also determine how much evidence is enough to clearly and confidently decide a student's proficiency level in each learning target.

Progress Toward Proficiency in Each Learning Target

By focusing on proficiency in grading, teachers naturally look to student growth. Since the ultimate goal in this system is to reach proficiency, there is no "banking," as in traditional grading. Traditionally, students could do well early on and coast to the finish line, cashing in their banked knowledge or, conversely, do poorly at first and never recover from past mistakes.

Again, the teacher can use the proficiency-based target like a sliding scale. As the student's proficiency increases, as suggested by the evidence, the teacher raises the proficiency score. If the evidence suggests a negative trend in learning, then he or she lowers the score.

Grading with proficiency keeps student performance in a state of flux. Students must *grow* to a specific level of competency and *maintain* that level. This fluidity not only increases the coursework's rigor but also increases the accountability to learn. It does so by engaging students in a framework that allows for continuous improvement.

Areas of Success and Growth

In evidence-based grading, teachers are concerned with a student's success and growth, and identifying these areas with students is essential. Since evidence is this system's focal point, teachers aim to make students aware of their growth and where their knowledge and skill development is taking them. Are they becoming more proficient? Less proficient? Are they stagnating?

It's also essential that teachers focus on students' successes and build on those successes to promote growth. Too many times we see deficiency models of grading and feedback that point to what students are lacking. Instead, we should show them what they are doing well, and we should lead them to positive growth and rewarding learning experiences.

When proficiency is the heart of the grading system, conversations become more *growth centered* and *positive in nature*. In traditional points-based grading, teachers concentrate on what the student did wrong. Since they take points away each time the student doesn't perform as expected, conversations tend to be negative and look backward. Focusing on proficiency tends to promote conversations based on what the student did correctly as well as *forward-facing feedback* or what the student can do next. These conversations are highly personalized, relevant, and more meaningful to students.

The proficiency-based learning target example in figure 1.4 demonstrates that each level of the gradation takes a positive viewpoint—what a student can or is able to do at that level. This focus on the positive creates a can-do culture. This means that the feedback teachers produce from student interactions with these types of proficiency-based learning targets is focused on where students are *succeeding* and how they can grow from where they are. Students react better when our feedback highlights their growth instead of what they didn't do or achieve.

Use Student-Produced Evidence

To successfully integrate evidence-based grading structures, teachers and school leaders must consider both grading and reporting practices. Is there a difference? Yes, there is a *huge* difference between reporting and grading. *Grading* is the act of interpreting, evaluating, and classifying student work in relation to collaboratively agreed-upon proficiency-based expectations. *Reporting* is the act of communicating student performance to stakeholders such as students, parents, and faculty. Many schools use evidence in their reporting practices but do not concern themselves with evidence in their grading practices.

While reporting changes may be necessary, unfortunately this is where many schools focus too much of their work. Bringing evidence into *both* grading and reporting is essential to successful implementation of evidence-based grading practices. Teams moving to evidence-based grading must understand that the change does not just apply to transcripts, progress reports, and report cards; it also applies to the way we teach, gather and interpret evidence from assessments, evaluate curriculum, and interact with students.

To get evidence to function properly in our grading system, we must understand how to properly integrate it into our grading and reporting practices, as table 1.1 shows.

Table 1.1: Integrating Evidence Into Grading and Reporting Practices

Integrating Evidence Into Grading Practices	Integrating Evidence Into Reporting Practices
Give feedback as the grade.	Apply gradations of learning.
Determine how well students should demonstrate new learning.	Focus on the student's body of work.
Search for evidence of growth.	Evaluate growth over time.
Co-construct learning with students.	Invite conversations.

Integrating Evidence Into Grading Practices

Evidence-based grading is the accurate interpretation of student performance. It relies essentially on a teacher's ability to recognize large- and small-scale patterns and hold contextualized conversations about emergent growth. As we note in table 1.1, the following strategies can help teachers integrate evidence into their grading practices.

Give Feedback as the Grade

As long as we're considering the possibility that letter grades are actually unproductive in the learning process, we also must consider what might fill the gap as a good replacement. We would argue that *narrative feedback* is one of the strongest contenders (Barnes, 2015). When evidence is the center of a grading model, the feedback, or a teacher's narrative on how a student is performing, becomes the ultimate prize.

When teachers analyze and interpret the evidence, they can use that evidence to guide future instruction. Who needs a grade when you can receive an articulated evaluation of your work? A single letter grade simply doesn't seem as useful to the learner.

Determine How Well Students Should Demonstrate New Learning

Evidence-based grading invites us to ask, "How well should students demonstrate new learning?" (Sandrock, 2011). When teachers build expectations into the language of the learning targets, the process of teaching and learning becomes a powerful interplay. With a focus on *how well*, the grading experience becomes more focused on thinking and growth.

Changing textbooks, rapidly evolving technology, and overdeveloped curricula force teachers cognitively further and further away from articulating their ideal expectations of students. This question of *how well* helps teachers articulate their expectations clearly and with intent, and openly vet expectations of student performance. This helps them grade their students more honestly, which leads to a more accurate assessment. Ultimately, this question of *how well* allows teachers to clearly define thresholds of quality and hold students accountable.

Search for Evidence of Growth

Teachers should attempt to capture more than just outcomes (answers) in their assessments within an evidence-based grading system. Evidence-based grading must measure growth as well. Thomas R. Guskey and Lee Ann Jung (2013) emphasize this mindset, stating, "Assessment must be seen as any process that captures a student's knowledge, ability, thinking and reactions at a particular point or points in time" (p. 17).

Using evidence in grading demands that teachers see learning from a growth perspective, and assessments must give them the chance to do so. Evidence-based grading defines *growth* as effective transformation of knowledge or skill into observable action. If assessments don't capture growth information, teachers simply are asking their students for mimicry, not mastery. Traditional grading focuses *only* on where a student's learning is. Evidence-based grading hinges on growth and requires assessments to be nimble, durable, and flexible to provide heavy contextual evidence of where a student's learning was, is, and might be headed.

Co-Construct Learning With Students

In evidence-based grading, teachers co-construct knowledge and skills with students. Because the teacher takes a position of *kinship* rather than *control*, students are more open to developing a trusting relationship with their teacher and are less likely to rationalize away critical feedback. Instead, students are more willing to use that feedback to gain an accurate perspective of their progress. With this co-constructivist approach, students' performance begins to match what they expect to happen. This alignment fosters confidence that allows growth to take hold and learning to occur more quickly.

Another advantage to the co-constructive stance is it allows student assessment to be more frequent and less invasive. This means the teacher is more of a researcher of learning, not a director of it (Elder, 2012). Being a *researcher* allows the teacher to call mindful attention to the learning targets while providing feedback to students. Learning becomes an *empowering* act and not simply mimicry.

During moments of co-construction, students can engage cognitively with their own learning, discuss evidence of learning with the teacher, and self-reflect on assessments.

Integrating Evidence Into Reporting Practices

Grading is one act; reporting grades is another. It can be challenging to report proficiency. The following sections explain how to improve reporting strategies to deliver proficiency information to students and their families.

Apply Gradations of Learning

Proficiency-based learning targets are important for learning but *essential* for evidence-based reporting. We define *proficiency-based learning targets* as successive degrees of competency that serve as a measurable learning outcome. A learning target, when used properly, represents a gradation of learning; teachers report a student's position on a particular gradation at a given point in learning. Since teachers base the gradebook on gradation levels, they must vet and create each gradation of a learning target. The most typical gradation structure is as follows.

1. **Has emerging understanding (gradation 1):** Students in this category may demonstrate basic levels of comprehension or skill development. Students may show growth that is disconnected from the target, or there is no pattern to their successes with the targets. Students regularly fail to meet one or more of the established targets (Guskey & Jung, 2013; Marzano, 2009; Moss & Brookhart, 2012).

2. **Approaches expectations (gradation 2):** Students in this category may inconsistently meet established targets and standards or may regularly fail to meet one or more of the established targets.

3. **Meets expectations (gradation 3):** Students in this category consistently meet requirements of the target and perform in a fully expected and reliable manner.

4. **Exceeds expectations (gradation 4):** Students in this category consistently and substantially exceed requirements and perform at maximum levels of effectiveness.

A gradation of learning creates a learning pathway for students to follow and a guide teachers can use to accurately report student performance.

Focus on the Student's Body of Work

Many schools, even with the support of expensive reporting software, do not base grading on a student's body of work. Instead, these schools continue to average performance, take the highest score and replace it with the most recent score, and use many other creative metrics to determine student performance. The fact remains that a student's body of work over time is the most reliable metric in determining overall student achievement.

This concept is similar to the process of building a resume. Over time, a student develops proficiency in areas of knowledge and skill, creating a resume of sorts. As the semester or year continues, students reevaluate this resume to determine their learning trajectory. This means they must connect their body of work (proficiency levels) to their potential growth and ultimately determine connections between what they are able to do now and what they can possibly do in the future. The teacher determines and reports the grade by connecting a student's body of work with growth.

Evaluate Growth Over Time

Allowing teachers the *time* they need to collect evidence is critical for evidence-based reporting. The reporting structure must accommodate this. A semester or yearlong time frame works best to accommodate adequate evidence collection. Teachers can use an evidence-based gradebook (see chapter 4, page 99) to break down all information about a student, as opposed to displaying a single mark. They can communicate information regarding growth, behavior, and achievement separately, creating a clear and complete learning profile. Collecting evidence in each area takes time.

Therefore, we must be patient with our reporting structure. This structure should have room for the time it takes to learn, patience with the assessment process, and pauses for quick and constant student evaluation.

Invite Conversations

If teachers simply implement evidence-based reporting by adapting the gradebook, nothing much will change in their conversations with students. Teachers may continue to focus, for example, on changing the exam questions based on the number of students who missed a particular question. But if we design the reporting structure to *support conversations*, then interaction with students supports growth and shifts from *reactive* to *proactive*. Mark Barnes (2015) notes, "If I were to sum it up in a single idea, my move to reject traditional grading occurred when I decided that engagement and conversations were to be the centerpieces of my teaching philosophy" (p. 40).

Teachers who commit to evidence-based reporting must frequently use gradebooks *during* instruction, mainly during reflection or the lesson's self-guided segments, to promote conversations about learning. Students should use gradebooks to identify strengths and weaknesses and prescribe future action rather than teachers allowing them to deduce that they are simply bad test takers or don't turn in homework. The manner in which teachers report evidence should attempt to invite conversations about learning, not minimize them.

In summary, to infuse our grading and reporting practices with evidence-based techniques, teachers and leaders alike must act empirically when engaging with student learning. This means that we must present well-founded research and experiential data that provide a basis for accurate instructional and grading practices and also promote informative reporting structures that rely on evidence of growth.

Key Points

As our team leaves the preparation phase of its journey, take the time to review the following key points from this chapter to ensure that you firmly grasp the content. Remember, the preparation phase simply introduces a new idea. As we move through the process of change, it is both smart and natural to return to the preparation phase to learn more, consider ideas differently, or read further about the idea you are working to implement.

- First, evidence-based grading means changing your practice. This is much different from reporting on standards, which simply means changing your gradebook.

- Second, we must change because the conversation about teaching and learning is changing. We must admit that preparing students for the 21st century demands a different approach to skill development—an approach that encourages continuous improvement, self-analysis, and mindful development.

- Third, evidence-based grading and reporting practices must, as the name states, always come back to evidence.

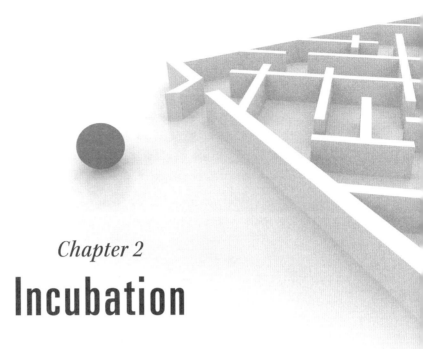

Chapter 2

Incubation

As our team moves forward from the preparation phase, it is important that it takes the time to fully understand the shift to evidence-based grading. Think time is often viewed as a luxury in education; however, the incubation phase is extremely valuable. It slows conversations and allows team members to flesh out their thinking in relation to the question, How is this best for students? This phase helps team members:

- Make smarter connections to the change concept and find the value in the work

- See the concept from their own angle

- Shape the concept in a way that is most valuable to teaching and learning practices

growth mindset

Sometimes, the incubation phase comes with pushback. It should. Change demands deliberation and debate. Pushback is a part of the change process, and it is part of what makes more valuable changes develop. Authentic buy-in is often the benefit of working through challenging and difficult conversations. For example, in the process of building change to an evidence-based grading model, many of our teacher teams found that they are able to sustain more specific and genuine conversations about the skills required in their disciplines.

For equity and fairness, learning development, and exploring how we nurture the potential of every student, an educational shift toward an evidence-based grading model makes good, smart sense. That said, it takes time and thoughtful leadership to allow this shift to take hold.

Following are three key points to remember during the incubation phase.

1. **Teachers must make sense of the change:** During this phase, teachers need time to allow the work done in the preparation phase to sink in. The time it takes to think and connect with a new idea is crucial to a more effective implementation of evidence-based grading.

2. **Anticipate pushback, confusion, and difficult conversations:** Teachers will see problems, concerns, and issues with making a change to evidence-based grading. They might see inconsistencies and misguided notions. They will question the change with smart and thoughtful intentions. Structure the dialogues these questions foster in a thoughtful way, and stay focused on the value this change can have in student learning, equity, skill development, and potential.

3. **Stick with the team during this phase:** Change in schools needs teacher leadership and support. Provide that support during the difficult exchanges, and keep the conversation going. Incubating ideas might sound like a frustrating debate at times, but change among thoughtful experts requires that. The keys here are that the team and each teacher continue to get supported during the change process and that ideas are valued in relation to what's best for students.

As you read the story about our team's experience in the incubation phase, notice how team members interact with both the *why* behind the change and *how* to implement the shift. Observe what kinds of ideas about grading practices are percolating. Consider the following questions as you read about how the team processes ideas about evidence-based grading.

- In what ways does the team realize how learning targets interact with an evidence-based grading approach? How does this approach to grading work with instruction?

- What questions do teachers ask while they brainstorm with one another? Do they come up with more obstacles or see the convincing advantages?

- Does the leadership hold the evidence-based grading concept to fidelity, or is the intention behind the change drifting?

Our Team's Story

Late in the summer, Mario and his team convene to begin final preparations on their conversion to evidence-based grading. During the preparation phase, his team examines the ideals and purposes of moving toward this new grading model.

It focuses on understanding the *why* behind the change, the thinking behind the change, and the significant shift from traditional grading practices. Mario wants his team to connect with the change by recognizing the value it brings to teaching and learning.

Their work the previous school year on the *why* of evidence-based grading provides them with a strong foundation for moving forward, and team members are motivated to do the hard work of implementation. That said, Kevin still struggles with letting go of the many years of traditional grading practices. He isn't 100 percent convinced.

On several occasions, Kevin says that he isn't sure the team should be doing this—he notes the confusion it might cause and the fact that very few schools are making the effort to change to evidence-based grading. He even notes how some schools tried and failed in their efforts.

As the team enters the room for its meeting, Kevin is still skeptical. Mario knows that it will be important to address Kevin's concerns. He values Kevin's thinking, and he knows it is important for the whole team to grapple with the questions—he is, after all, asking the questions any thoughtful educator might ask.

Mario begins the meeting. "At this point in our work, I think it's important to revisit our rationale for moving to evidence-based grading, but I also think we should take a close look at the obstacles and concerns that might stand in the way. If we are going to move in this direction, we need to make sure we are convinced about the advantages and can explain the change to anyone with questions about the work we are doing.

"In May, Kevin asked some excellent questions we need to address, and he identified a number of concerns. Let's start thinking about this work and brainstorming. Then we can think through any points we need to address."

"Mario, it isn't that I don't believe in these changes," Kevin says, "but I still don't know whether they are worth implementing. Is it worth all the work? This change is unlike other changes we've tried. Most people seem to think that our current grading practices make sense, so why would we want to make a disruptive change like this?"

Maya replies, "I understand what you're saying, Kevin. I'm wondering, do you think you don't understand the reason well enough, or do you think implementing it would just be too much for students and parents to understand in a meaningful way?"

"I understand the shift in principle," Kevin says, "but putting it into practice worries me. I think it will confuse our students and parents. As hard as it is to accept, it is clear that our current grading system is inequitable. I see why the shift could help us implement more equitable grading practices to help students; however, I'm not sure if the impact is worth the work and possible confusion it will cause. If we focus more on our discussion of teaching and learning, isn't that more interesting to all of us? I think discussions about instruction help students more than discussions about feedback and grades."

Mario listens closely to what Kevin is saying. Every team member views Kevin as a mentor.

Kevin continues, "I mean, isn't evidence-based grading just a collection of the best practices that we use on a daily basis? We have always known that quality learning targets and great feedback are essential, and formative assessments are great tools to collect evidence of student learning. I don't know . . . it just seems like all this evidence-based stuff is what we do anyway. Why confuse things with a shift in our grading practices?"

"I sort of agree," Britney says. "When we met in May to talk about evidence-based grading, I was excited! But as I thought about it, I realized we were doing all that stuff already. I'm not sure I see how this change is going to make much more of an impact, but I do see how it might confuse our students."

Britney and Joni join Kevin and Maya on their side of the table, and Mario senses their hesitation about moving forward. His team sees the obstacles, and he knows that these concerns are legitimate.

"I agree that we use all these practices really well, but moving to evidence-based grading is also a change to the gradebook," Mario says. "It reflects how we approach our teaching practices and make our expectations clear. When I think about the gradebook, I like to think about it as a way to open up stronger discussions about teaching and learning and what we expect of our students. I agree with you, Kevin. I think the change will be disruptive initially, but I think the end results are worth the effort."

"Yes, but even so, in the end we have to give students a grade. If it's a 4, 3, 2, or 1, I'm not seeing how that is different from an A, B, C, or D," Kevin says. "If I don't understand that, I don't think my students will, and I'm sure their parents won't. The only discussions we'll have will focus on changes in the gradebook, and if a 4 is really just an A and a 3 is really just a B. Those discussions might get us sidetracked from the conversations we want to have about instruction and how students can learn."

"I know it's a difficult approach to implement," Mario says, "but let's think back on our other discussions. It sounds like we need to revisit our thinking.

For instance, during our last meeting, we discussed that letter grades communicate very little or perhaps nothing to the learner. That is a mistake I don't want to knowingly repeat. We felt this way because behind the letter grade, there is nothing more than points and percentages categorized by tests, homework, and participation—categories that do not communicate anything specific about our expectations for learning. We decided it is our job to make the gradebook more informative to the learner and more specific about how we communicate our expectations. A better gradebook could provide clarity in how we communicate about learning and student growth."

"But why does that need to be in the gradebook?" Kevin asks. "Why can't we just do that in class like we've been doing for years?"

"Well," Mario says, "one difference might be that the gradebook could capture the conversations we have with students. Gradebooks based on learning goals or targets could benefit the learner if we build them differently. Then students could see their growth in learning over time. They could map out their learning, visibly see their strengths, and clearly identify learning gaps."

Britney says, "If we keep a categorical, points-based system in our gradebook, it only sorts students and does nothing to provide actionable feedback for them to understand how to succeed. They just have a running list of numbers, not a growth chart of skills. The traditional gradebook does not give students or parents the words to start a conversation about learning."

"OK, so let's say that the targets are in the gradebook, and we give students a 4, 3, 2, or 1 score. Let's focus on how that helps," Joni says.

Mario says, "I see why this is difficult. Remember, we should not think of 4, 3, 2, and 1 as numbers. They have no numerical value. They simply act as markers that represent student skill development relative to an expected performance or outcome. Because students can see their aptitude and growth trends, they can more clearly understand their strengths and weaknesses. More important, they can see how those strengths and weaknesses trend toward achievement. Currently, our gradebooks are just point tallies. How many times have you heard a student say, 'I am only fifteen points away from getting an A'? We need to hear, 'I am these three skills away from reaching proficiency or mastery.'"

Maya says, "I see how this might help the student, but it is harder for us to grade. We have to go into the gradebook and enter all the numbers for each test."

"Well, not really," Joni says. "Since we are grading with learning targets, we do not give a 4 for a test. Instead, we check the test to see what targets it is aligned with, identify the questions that relate to each target, and give a score for each target that the student had."

Mario says, "When we grade this way, we can be very clear about where students struggle, and this should help inform immediate changes to our instructional practices."

"I see this can have some advantages, but we still need to give term grades," Kevin says. "Every six weeks, we have to identify targets in the gradebook to arrive at a grade."

Mario replies, "I know, but we could allow the gradebook to be open all semester. There would be no term or quarter grades."

The group sits silent for a moment, and then Kevin says, "Well, that's nice. I like that. That would give students more time to learn."

Mario lets everyone think on that point for a moment as he distributes an excerpt from *On Your Mark* (Guskey, 2015).

Mario says, "In this text, Guskey states that grades must be based on three components: progress, process, and product. *Progress* is the student's growth of skill and knowledge, *process* is the student's behavior and attitude, and *product* is the result produced by the student from the synthesis of his or her knowledge and skills. This is what must be in our gradebook. Right now, we have product and process meshed together, and progress is nowhere to be found."

Maya says, "We do have growth. Students can see their grades and test scores go up or down each term."

"Yeah, but they can't deduce anything about their learning from that," Joni replies. "They might think they are just bad test takers or that they are just not good at mathematics. I don't think our current gradebooks give students the words they need to understand their learning."

Mario has one last thought. "Remember, the gradebook must help students understand themselves as *learners*. To achieve that goal, the gradebook must align with what is happening in class—feedback, dynamic instruction, and constant and consistent assessment, not point accumulation. When would we ever say to a student, 'Great job! You learned 17.5 points better on that activity; now you are an A student'?"

The team laughs, and Kevin concedes, "All right. I absolutely get your point. So, how do we set this up?"

Mario proceeds to lay out the plan to officially begin implementing evidence-based grading. While team members feel a bit hesitant, they also realize that this is the right work to finally create a learning-focused curriculum.

The Four Unexpected Relationships in Evidence-Based Grading

The cycle of inquiry never ends when we work in a collaborative culture. Collaborative cultures seek continual improvement. Unexpected observations, questions, connections, and ideas constantly emerge. Our team members always seek improvement—they want to do the right thing for students, so they consider all ideas carefully. In this part of our team's story, the team pushes itself beyond the basic understanding of a learning target and works to determine how well students are succeeding. It considers evidence that proves developing success.

As our team members shift their collaborative conversations to *how well* a student meets a proficiency expectation, they begin to question their instructional practices' effectiveness in helping students navigate a gradation of learning. The team moves away from past conversations that identified students' work as right or wrong and instead concentrates on evidence that students produce.

During the incubation phase, it is easy for teams to get sidetracked. They are still learning, grappling with new ideas, and figuring out how to make those new ideas work effectively. Some team members may process the change differently, with different perceptions and different confrontations. They begin to view their learning targets through a proficiency lens, which leads them to reflect on other significant challenges and ideas about teaching and learning. In this phase, the team needs supportive leadership as it shifts its traditional focus from right and wrong to describing how well students perform.

Teams typically discover important unexpected relationships during their evidence-based grading journey. It is critical that team members continue to push each other's thinking about the unexpected combinations within the evidence-based grading framework. Before a team can move on to grading in an evidence-based system, it should remember the following four unexpected relationships.

1. Proficiency-based learning targets connect with grading.

2. Feedback connects with instruction.

3. Assessment connects with grading.

4. The gradebook connects with learning.

Proficiency-Based Learning Targets Connect With Grading

The *exchange of a performance for feedback* is grading's most basic function. This exchange is a major principle of evidence-based grading: a learner performing with feedback as the reward and nothing else. This is a difficult idea, but we can understand it more clearly by comprehending the purpose of proficiency-based learning targets as it relates to evidence-based grading.

O'Connor (2009) states, "Grades must be directly related to the learning goals" (p. 47). We take this to mean that proficiency-based learning targets are essential to an effective grading system. Learning targets are the mechanism for collecting evidence of performance, providing feedback, and creating proper assessments. Since the learning target is so essential to grading in an evidence-based grading system, the system depends on the target's quality. To ensure teachers build quality proficiency-based learning targets, we must make sure learning targets are:

- **Clear**—Learning targets must be written in a clear way so that students understand them.

- **Rigorous**—Learning targets should express the rigor of expectation.

- **Scaled**—Learning targets should be scaled in a way that clearly describes performance.

- **Assessed**—Learning targets should be assessed against clearly defined expectations.

Proficiency-Based Learning Targets Must Be Clear

Specificity might be considered a synonym for *clarity*. When it comes to evidence-based grading, this is not necessarily true. In evidence-based grading, to be clear means to articulate proficiency. Simply put, if targets are clear, everybody easily understands what *proficient* means.

Adding more details doesn't mean we communicate a learning target more clearly. Let's look at two examples from a fifth-grade mathematics class. In the first example, the learning target attempts to be clear by adding more *specific* details.

> I can write, interpret, and explain both algebraic and numerical expressions by using operation symbols for addition, subtraction, and multiplication.

The second example's learning target attempts to be more specific through *proficiency-based* language.

> I can *accurately* write numerical expressions in *familiar* situations using *relevant* operation symbols.

When teachers write learning targets using proficiency-based language, the resulting targets invite students to think about their performance differently so they know what they need to achieve and the differences among needing to improve, proficiency, and mastery. As we continue to develop our ability to articulate these differences, it is important to remember that the verb (what you want the student to know, understand, or do) doesn't change; proficiency-based language articulates the *quality* of student performance. From there, teachers then evaluate the student's demonstrated performance relative to the clarified statement of proficiency.

Proficiency-Based Learning Targets Must Be Rigorous

Rigorous might be considered a synonym for *difficult*. We don't see rigor that way. In an evidence-based world, we see rigor as the perfect balance between challenge and capacity, which is essential to scaling targets and ultimately grading students (Wiliam, 2011). Rigor essentially is the *desirable difficulty level* of learning (Brown, Roediger, & McDaniel, 2014).

Each gradation of a proficiency-based learning target must represent the level of performance students must achieve that represents a "stretch success." When students stretch for success, they see the next gradation of their learning as an attainable goal, which means they need to learn or practice how to get there (Brown et al., 2014). A learning target is essentially a gradation of rigor for what we want a student to be able to know, understand, or do in a course of study.

Proficiency-Based Learning Targets Must Be Scaled

All learning happens on a gradation, which is best articulated through proficiency-based language. Rarely can a person lack a skill, then still lack the skill, and then suddenly acquire the skill! Learning occurs slowly and sometimes unconsciously. Then, learning "clicks" as knowledge, understanding, or skill.

Think about it. Does a child progress directly from crawling to walking? Does a dancer progress immediately from first position to performing ballet? These examples of learning and development take place on a gradation, incrementally changing and growing from a current state of learning to a new state of learning. Learning expectations (proficiency-based learning targets) act in the same way. They are essentially *gradations of quality* anchored to an *idea of growth*.

When writing proficiency-based targets, many teachers state, "First, have students list the words, then have them define the words, then they can explain the words, and so on." While this seems logical, it is actually an incorrect way to approach learning targets and grading. In order to properly function on a gradation of quality, each gradation of the learning target must be positioned in relation to what is expected from the student. A gradation must focus on a single skill. We highlight this idea with the concept of shadows. Look at figure 2.1. What do you notice about the cast shadow?

Figure 2.1: Cast shadow.

You may notice that while there is a cast shadow, the front of the sphere reflects light, ranging from dark black to light gray until the shadow is completely gone. More important, you may notice that the shadow's shape is the shape of the ball! The shadow is not a square or triangle; the shadow is the same shape as the object. This is similar to how a learning target gradation works.

All learning target gradations must relate to one another because they are all shadows of the same expectation. If I asked a child to learn how to ride a bike, a gradation of that task might be, "Ride a bike with training wheels." It would not be, "List all the parts of the bike and define how they work."

Just as the shadow is a gradation of the reflected light from the ball, learning targets reflect the competency that each level in the learning gradation outlines. The problem is that some educators attempt to implement evidence-based grading formed on learning progressions instead of learning targets. Learning progressions are scaled gradations of learning; however, each gradation is a different proficiency expectation—the numbers correspond with the level of proficiency achieved. For example:

> 4—Analyze familiar and structured situations using relevant vocabulary, context, and details.
>
> 3—Explain the appropriate details in familiar and structured situations.
>
> 2—Define the appropriate vocabulary, details, and context in familiar and structured situations.
>
> 1—Identify the appropriate vocabulary, details, and context in familiar and structured situations.

While this example is a gradation of learning, each gradation level is not the same action or application. Notice that each level is a different proficiency expectation. Gradation 1 is *identify*, and gradation 3 is *explain*. Creating learning targets in this way may lead to an unsuccessful implementation of evidence-based grading. Successful implementation must use learning targets with the same action or application in each gradation, as in the following learning target gradation example.

4—Independently create an appropriate spoken message in unfamiliar and unstructured situations.

3—Independently create an appropriate spoken message in familiar and unstructured situations.

2—Independently create an appropriate spoken message in familiar and structured situations.

1—Independently attempt to create an appropriate spoken message in familiar and structured situations.

Notice that each gradation is a version (shadow) of gradation 3. This is essential for successful evidence-based grading implementation.

Some might think that the best students can do is what teachers ask of them—gradation 3. However, in order for evidence-based grading to function properly, a teacher must visualize and articulate what may lie beyond one's expectations of mastery. We should not only work for student success at a level of proficiency; we want *all* students to be challenged, meaning that those who demonstrate proficiency are not finished learning—we must support their learning to exceed proficiency and gain mastery.

Look back at figure 2.1. Any good art student will tell you that to properly outline an image, one must think about the shadow *on all sides of the object*. Note how the sphere casts a large shadow behind it, but it also casts a small amount of reflected light shadow in front.

This small front shadow is the equivalent of *exceeds mastery* in evidence-based learning targets, or level 4. We don't consider this gradation the place students must get to but rather a learning space where students can enrich their proficiency.

The proficiency-based learning gradation is important; without this gradation, it would be impossible to identify growth and provide actionable feedback to students.

Proficiency-Based Learning Targets Must Be Assessed

Teachers can assess every learning target in a number of ways. Therefore, we must create the appropriate assessment portfolio to capture the correct evidence and accurately rate students (O'Connor, 2009). To properly assess students, teachers should use scaled learning targets to create assessments, so the assessments are evaluated against the gradation of the proficiency stated in the learning target. Figure 2.2 shows how aligning and balancing assessment and stated proficiency are important.

Teachers should aim assessment at gradation 3 of the learning target with opportunities for extension (gradation 4) as well as verification of the target's remedial levels (gradations 1 and 2). If teachers do not align the target to assessments in this way, then they may not be able to use the evidence that students produce, they may receive misguided feedback about the learner, or worse, they may misclassify student performance.

Feedback Connects With Instruction

We know that effective feedback is a crucial element of teaching and learning. An evidence-based grading model focuses on feedback and its role in developing instruction—pointing the learner in a specific direction of growth.

Figure 2.2: Aligned and balanced assessment.

The Purpose of Feedback in Evidence-Based Grading

In traditional classrooms and grading systems, teachers typically provide feedback separately from grades. They often see sidebar conversations, checks for understanding, or exit slips as feedback. These check-ins are often grounded in a teacher's perception rather than the evidence students demonstrate. In an effective evidence-based grading model, *feedback is the grade* (Barnes, 2015). As we move away from points, averages, and letter grades, students must interact with feedback as the reference point for how they are performing and how they can improve.

In evidence-based grading, the teacher gives a letter grade to represent the level to which a student accepts, implements, and grows from feedback. When the teacher provides feedback in relation to a proficiency expectation, the student gains a clear picture of his or her current state of understanding. Feedback simply provides a stable and clear frame of reference from which to learn (O'Connor, 2009). This type of feedback gives students simultaneous perspective and advice on improvement.

What Feedback Looks Like in Evidence-Based Grading

In his session at the Global Leadership Summit in 2015, Capella Hotel Group CEO Horst Schulze suggested that world-class customer service is reliable, timely, and caring. While we are not in the hotel or retail business, we *are* in the customer service business. We need to be clear and reliable with students as they are working to meet the expectations of a rigorous curriculum. Our students are our customers. We should view student feedback through a similar lens. In an evidence-based grading model, feedback must be *unbiased*, *actionable*, and *accepted*.

Unbiased Feedback

What a teacher says to students in the form of feedback is more important than the assessment itself. It probably goes without saying that teachers must provide feedback of the highest quality. If we are not careful, feedback to students can become distorted, misinterpreted, rationalized, or even unwanted (Schoemaker, 2011).

Feedback can become distorted when the communication between student and teacher results in misperception, misapplication of skills or knowledge, or even nonlearning—times when we see no learning growth or worse, negative growth. The following list of questions, adapted from the work of decision science and behavioral economics expert Paul J. H. Schoemaker (2011), outlines how teachers can ensure their feedback is high quality.

- **Is the feedback biased?** Do you have any preconceptions about the student that may cause you to *assume* why he or she got an answer right or wrong? Preconceptions cause feedback to be unreliable. The challenge is to make feedback informative and evaluative but not biased.

- **Does the feedback have context?** Is your feedback based on an unfamiliar or unrelated context, or is it in line with what students expect to focus on?

- **Are the students ready?** Do your lessons allow students to prepare to receive feedback? Feedback should not come as a surprise to students. Best teaching practices clarify expectations early, provide formative feedback during the learning process, and create a growth-minded learning environment in which students are capable of giving and receiving supportive feedback. Students who know how their performance will be evaluated are well positioned to receive feedback and constructive criticism.

- **What data does the feedback rely on?** Does your feedback rely on the most readily available data or a full data set of student performance? Partial or incorrect data can cause untrustworthy feedback.

- **Is the feedback clear?** Do you use language that makes it clear how you want students to grow in learning, or do you use only deficiency language? In other words, do your expectations frame growth potential by stating what proficient work *does* look like, or do your expectations state what proficient work *does not* look like?

- **Is the feedback balanced?** Does your feedback evaluate both the performance of the skill and the quality of the learning?

- **Is the feedback relevant?** Does the feedback relate to the learning target? Does it contain the aspects of proficiency from the learning target?

In evidence-based grading, teachers think about their feedback often and scrutinize it to the same level that they scrutinize student performance. At this point, team members who collaborate with one another to consistently assess student work calibrate their expectations of student performance and offer a much more equitable feedback experience across the team. This collaboration and auditing of each other's interpretation of student work ensures that feedback becomes clearer, more understandable, and more valuable. Calibrating what is being communicated to a student ensures that the student more readily accepts feedback and lessens the probability that the information will be misinterpreted or rationalized away.

Actionable Feedback

Feedback that doesn't invite action is meaningless (Wiliam, 2011). If you gave a friend advice, and he or she does nothing with your feedback, wouldn't you feel like your words meant nothing? In evidence-based grading, actions must be the result of feedback. Teachers should focus on prescriptive, reactive, and inclusive feedback instead of feedback that focuses on student deficiencies.

Prescriptive feedback tells a student how to turn his or her current state of learning into an expectation (Wiliam, 2011). *Reactive feedback*, on the other hand, comments on past performance by telling students what went wrong. Prescriptive feedback possesses forward-facing language that provides the learner with a clear message and the pathway to the next level on the proficiency scale. Dylan Wiliam (2011) describes this idea as creating a *feedback loop*. By combining prescription with reaction, we can create these loops successfully.

Reactive feedback might sound like:

- "Manny, you didn't do so well on the World War I section of the quiz. Let's look at why you missed those questions."

- "Tara, your vocabulary quiz didn't go so well. Let's find out what words you missed and practice those flashcards."

Prescriptive feedback may sound like:

- "Manny, I noticed that you keep forgetting to include the main cause of World War I. That detail will certainly enhance your work."

- "Tara, just add a few more of those vocabulary words we talked about, and those words will help focus your presentation on the theme more! You are almost there!"

Inclusive feedback is essential to promote learning. Inclusive feedback means that the student must work through positive criticism to realize his or her growth. Because learning is highly personal and challenging, students may think they are unable to achieve if they receive negative or deficient feedback. Remember, the language of feedback must always center on what the student *is doing* and *can do*. This drives learning forward, inviting the student to see his or her own emerging ability. Inclusive feedback might sound like:

- "Amber, your writing includes so many great details, and you do an excellent job of adding in your opinion about this topic. Take that same strength and apply it to a few more areas in your writing to round out this work."

- "Jake, look at how far you have come in your knowledge about maps! You are starting to associate the state capitals well. Keep it going."

Accepted Feedback

While it is important to provide actionable feedback, that won't matter if the student doesn't accept and trust the feedback. In traditional grading systems, students often look past all the feedback to the letter grade or points earned. In an evidence-based model, students must read the feedback to understand how well they demonstrated proficiency.

Additionally, students must *trust* the feedback they receive. If they trust the feedback and understand it in relation to the learning target, they are more likely to act on it, revise their efforts, and hone their skills. In an evidence-based grading system, we must be sure students understand and accept feedback. Only then will it lead to learning growth and development. Grant Wiggins (2010) articulates the same idea. He states that feedback is communication about "what the learner did and did not do in relation to [learning] goals. . . . It empowers the student to make intelligent adjustments when [he or she] applies it to [the] next attempt to perform" (Wiggins, 2010).

In "What's Worth an 'A'? Setting Standards Together," Doris Sperling (1993) suggests that in formative assessment experiences, "criteria are clearly spelled out, [so] students can take responsibility to evaluate their own work" (p. 73). The more students experience feedback coming from their own thinking, as co-constructed or self-generated, the more likely they are to trust it and use it to improve their learning. Cris Tovani (2012) asserts, "The feedback students give is just as important as the feedback they get" (p. 48).

Teachers should begin the feedback process with what we call *nonevaluative conversations* with students to create unbiased and actionable feedback that students accept. The conversations this process evokes will ensure that feedback is highly relevant, prepares students to receive the feedback positively, and increases the chance that they trust and act on the feedback. These conversations also create an exchange where feedback flows from teacher to student and back from student to teacher. As this exchange matures, the student-teacher feedback relationship builds a strong foundation from which quality feedback can help a student grow.

For example, suppose a parent is evaluating a child's drawing of a cat. The first thing a parent says is not, "Great job, but relative to all the cat drawings done by children your age, this isn't that great. I would call this average to below-average work." No. The parent says, "Wow, this is really good! Why did you make its ears that shape? Why did you draw it on this part of the page? What is the cat doing?" These are all nonevaluative comments that invite feedback from the child and create a quality foundation for communication.

Nonevaluative conversations might sound like the following.

- "How does that word you used capture the point you are trying to make?"
- "Tell me how you approached solving that problem."
- "What are you trying to say in your work that is relevant to your audience?"
- "Is your work believable to another person reading it?"
- "What assumptions would another person be able to make about your work?"

Experts like Susan Brookhart in her book *Learning Targets: Helping Students Aim for Understanding in Today's Lesson* (Moss & Brookhart, 2012) and Dylan Wiliam (2011) in his book *Embedded Formative Assessment* have exhaustive lists of these types of questions that will help support nonevaluative conversations with students. These conversations are essential to producing the quality feedback we have discussed, as they point the learner toward growth.

Assessment Connects With Grading

As we learn more about how to use evidence of student proficiency as assessment and grading's primary driver, we are convinced that assessment has become the new language of learning. Teachers shouldn't design assessments simply to prove what students are or are not learning; they should use assessments to show students their progress and how to improve on it. "The purpose of classroom assessment [must now be] to inform learning, not to sort and select or justify a grade" (McTighe & Ferrara, 2000, p. 11).

In order for assessments to inform learning, it is important that teachers design the assessment structure to reveal all that it should about a student's learning. As Guskey and Jung (2013) write, "Assessment in education is any process used to gather information about student learning, that is, what students know, are able to do, and believe at a particular point in time" (p. 17). This statement challenges us to verify whether our assessments are as revealing as they should be. Do they tell both the teacher and the learner everything they need to know? Are they trustworthy?

Guskey and Jung's (2013) point drives us to the essential question on assessment in the incubation phase: Are our assessments revelatory enough? Ultimately, this question prompts us to ask ourselves, "Do we know as much about our students as we think we do?" Assessments must provide a complete learning snapshot. This picture serves as the class's instructional foundation and allows for quality feedback.

In evidence-based grading, assessment quality checklists similar to the following can help teachers create *revelatory assessments*—those that reveal how students grow, how they apply their thinking, and how they attempt to grow from their thinking (Ainsworth & Viegut, 2006).

- Do our questions gather evidence of proficiency?
- Do the assessment's components collect evidence on other gradations of the learning target? That is to say, does the assessment allow students to demonstrate the range of their abilities?
- Is there enough evidence to determine proficiency?
- How much time do we need to interact with the assessment?
- Does the assessment's size correlate to the size of the necessary conversation about the topic? (The larger or more in-depth the conversation, the smaller the assessment needed.)
- Does the assessment produce evidence of student perceptions, thinking patterns, and mental maps?
- Does the assessment allow us as well as the student to see growth?

Notice that the term *right answer* is missing from this list. In evidence-based grading, assessment is less concerned about verifying right answers and more concerned with verifying *right thinking*. Teachers can use these questions to ensure that their assessments verify a healthy balance between right thinking and right answers.

This list includes questions that verify the assessment's effectiveness after teachers have created it—something we think educators don't talk about enough. As we've seen with the teams we work with, these questions help ensure that every assessment captures the necessary information or data about students. One teacher told us that she loves these questions. She went on to explain that there are so many lists out there that provide a formula or steps about how to *create* common assessments, but there are not many lists that outline how to *check the quality and validity* of the assessments we have already created.

The big idea in the incubation phase is that teachers shift from the question, How do I collect evidence that students learned the content? to How do I collect evidence that students understand *how they attempt to make sense* of the content? For this reason, teachers must view assessment differently than they may be used to and make some critical assessment decisions.

First, teachers must decide which assessments they can use as evidence. In evidence-based grading, formative assessments must be plentiful. However, with so much formative assessment going on, it is hard for students to determine what teachers use as evidence and what they don't. It is important for teachers to clearly delineate what is usable evidence (for teacher evaluation and judgment) and what is merely formative (for self-assessment).

Once teachers have decided on which assessments to use for student proficiency, they must decide on a *performance window*, the time period in which all eligible evidence may be used to show proficiency. There must be a window of time in which all evidence created is open for teacher interpretation. Teachers can ask themselves the following three questions in order to create performance windows.

1. **"When do I need to know where students are?"** The assessment's timing in an evidence-based curriculum is critical to successful implementation. Assessing too much or too little is less important than assessing at exactly the right point in the learning. For example, summative experiences that occur sooner in the lesson plan are a better option than leaving them for the end. Performance windows are essential to the proper function of evidence-based grading, and teachers must communicate to the students what these windows are.

2. **"How will I judge student evidence?"** Within these performance windows, teachers may grapple with the idea of diagnostic assessments versus evaluative assessments. Teachers should ask themselves, "Are my assessments diagnostic? Do they provide feedback about what is going on within the student performance, or do they evaluate the performance?"

To judge evidence effectively, a teacher must use all types of assessments, including informal observations, dialogue with students, exams, learning tasks, and performance-based events, to name a few.

3. **"How much evidence do I need for accurate assessment?"**
Assessment provides an opportunity for students to apply new learning and to self-judge whether they are consolidating that new learning. Finding this balance is key to successful assessment and working toward growth for all learners.

The Gradebook Connects With Learning

Educators are asking more from the gradebook. In the past, the gradebook was simply a teacher's journal in which only the teacher saw his or her students' grades, and students waited for a single letter grade at the end of a term. The gradebook's original purpose was to inform the teacher how to create the final grade. The students never got a glimpse into this secret book. Using the handwritten gradebook was common practice until the early 2000s when technology advancements brought gradebooks online.

Technology outpaced the way we think about gradebooks. Now, students, parents, counselors, deans, and principals can and must view the information in the gradebook to assess and support students. With so many eyes on the gradebook, its functionality is fundamentally different from years past. The main change is that all parties are silently demanding that the gradebook provide as much information about each learner as possible (O'Connor, 2009; Willis, 1993).

Gradebooks remain unchanged simply because they have been "good enough." Teachers change only their instruction and assessment to align with best practice. While changing instruction to align with quality formative learning principles is necessary, the gradebook must come along as well. To encourage teachers to create evidence-based gradebooks, we invite them to think about gradebooks differently. An evidence-based gradebook should accomplish the following five goals (Willis, 1993).

1. Generate an instructional purpose.
2. Focus on proficiency-based learning targets.
3. Align language with instruction.
4. Evaluate student growth potential.
5. Separate student behavior from academic performance.

Generate an Instructional Purpose

Some teachers base their gradebooks solely on accumulating points from a set of tasks, which says nothing about any skills the student is developing. In traditional gradebooks like these, which use total points grouped into categories such as *tests*, *quizzes*, *participation*, *homework*, and so on, students may only deduce that they are bad or good test takers, whether they work hard, or whether they have turned in all their homework.

Alternatively, students can open an evidence-based gradebook and deduce that they lack a skill, such as *creates a valid argument*, *cites details from a text*, or *writes a thesis correctly*. Teachers can only provide this type of information when they base the gradebook on learning targets. This foundation helps the learner and all parties target interventions, provide self-reflection, and differentiate instruction. Teachers can successfully insert a gradebook structured around learning targets into the lesson with immediate instructional value for students. It encourages instruction and assessment to "talk to each other." The gradebook must have a purpose in instruction. Teachers might ask themselves the following questions to decide how to use their gradebooks to inform instruction (Guskey & Jung, 2013).

- What information do I communicate to students during instruction?

- When a student needs intervention, what information would be useful to my colleagues?

- Is the information in my gradebook usable for instructional change?

If a teacher can answer these questions sufficiently, he or she can structure the gradebook to generate an instructional purpose—a much more informative communication tool for student achievement.

Focus on Proficiency-Based Learning Targets

Wiggins (1996) states that "what critics of grading must understand is that the symbol [the grade] is not the problem; the lack of stable and clear points of reference in using symbols is the problem" (p. 142). This means that grades are not the enemy, but the gradebook lacks clear evidence for the learner to use to understand the grade. This is why an evidence-based gradebook must be based on learning targets that act as clear points of reference for students.

Evidence-based gradebooks should articulate the expectations for learning. "If grading does not relate grades back to standards [targets], they are giving a mixed message. Our grading practice must reflect and illuminate standards [targets]" (O'Connor, 2009, p. 12). Sadly, most gradebooks are based on methods of assessment (O'Connor, 2009). Figure 2.3 shows the traditional point system and categories separated by homework, quizzes, projects, and tests with total points listed in parentheses. All these types of assessments may be important, but if they do not provide information about learning, then they offer very little useful information.

Student	Grade	Percentage	Homework			Quizzes				Projects		Tests	
			Homework Week 1 (10)	Homework Week 2 (2)	Homework Week 3 (16)	Quiz 1 (20)	Quiz 2 (20)	Quiz 3 (20)	Quiz 4 (20)	Project 1 (40)	Project 2 (40)	Test 1 (100)	Test 2 (100)
Chris	A	94.4	10	2	16	17	20	18	19	37	39	94	95
Selena	A	93.1	8	2	16	16	19	18	19	36	40	93	91
Jason	C	76.3	8	0	13	15	17	18	12	30	35	80	71
Min	B	85.7	7	2	14	18	16	17	16	37	35	80	85

Figure 2.3: Traditional point system and categories.

In order for students to self-assess effectively, learning targets—not categories of tasks, such as quizzes, projects, or tests—must be in the gradebook. The learning target is the language we use during the lesson to tell students how to improve; we must see that same language in the gradebook.

When gradebooks are based on learning targets instead of marks or points, we have effectively created a learning cycle, which means students don't have to step aside to receive feedback in the classroom or to suddenly make inferences about themselves from a letter grade. They can simply see the same feedback that occurred during the learning process in the gradebook itself.

Basing the gradebook on learning targets can be difficult, as many teachers have not conceptualized what that actually looks like. For example, an evidence-based gradebook might look like figure 2.4 (page 66).

This example is very different from traditional gradebooks based on points or percentages. Instead, the evidence-based gradebook shows numbers from 1 to 4 and communicates how a student performed on a learning target, not an assessment. In the actual gradebook, events are named.

	Standard 1										
	Learning Target 1			Learning Target 2				Learning Target 3			
Student	Event 1	Event 2	Event 3	Event 1	Event 2	Event 3	Event 4	Event 1	Event 2	Event 3	Event 4
Chris	2	2	3	3	3	4	3	3	3	4	3
Selena	3	3	3	3	3	3	2	3	3	3	3
Jason	2	1	3	3	2	2	2	1	2	2	2
Min	3	2	3	3	2	2	2	3	3	2	3

Figure 2.4: Evidence-based system and categories.

The most difficult concept to grasp might be that the numbers have no numerical value. The numbers are merely positional markers on a gradation of learning. It might be more helpful to think about these numbers like those on an elevator—they represent the floor or level, not whether the passenger (student) got four points for arriving at the fourth floor.

Align Language With Instruction

Information in the gradebook represents the teacher's complete professional judgment of a learner. When a student looks in the gradebook, he or she should see language aligned with language the teacher uses regularly during instruction and throughout formative assessment. When the language of the classroom aligns with the language of the gradebook, students won't see a grade of 95 percent or 70 percent; they will see the language of learning that they've been working to achieve in class. In this way, the assessment and reporting process mirrors curricular and instructional classroom expectations.

If our gradebooks were structured the way we talk with students about learning and expectations in class, we would see teachers speaking to students about their competencies and proficiencies: "Try this skill and you will succeed" or "Remember that you didn't have a good grasp of this concept; get that down and you will improve." This is the language of learning from the classroom, and an evidence-based gradebook should mirror that language.

Evaluate Student Growth Potential

When the teacher bases the gradebook on proficiencies, students should be able to quickly and clearly identify their strengths and weaknesses to know where and how to improve. Gradebooks must be able to communicate growth. Guskey (2015) states that we must have a progress grade along with process and product. The *growth indicator*, as one of our teachers calls it, is a measure that states whether the student is meeting all the curriculum's development challenges. In evidence-based grading, we use the growth report in figure 2.5 to communicate this critical piece of information.

Key: AG = Adequate growth MG = Minimal growth F = Failure to grow I = Insufficient evidence	
Student Name	**Weekly Growth Score**
Mohammad	AG
Sarah	MG
John	F
Suzie	I

Figure 2.5: Weekly growth report.

Adequate growth means students are progressing through all the course's developmental challenges. Adequate growth is important because a student of any aptitude can grow, something a traditional outcome-based grading model simply doesn't support or promote. Evidence-based grading promotes growth and states that any student can and will grow because it provides the opportunities to do so.

One of an evidence-based system's most important elements is that it allows a teacher to indicate growth even though the student's aptitude may be low. In other words, it gives the teacher the flexibility to observe and monitor growth. The gradebook should be able to reflect this growth in learning.

Next, *minimal growth* is an important identifier, as it might have eligibility or response to intervention implications. In a smarter, evidence-based grading system, teachers monitor students closely so they can implement interventions for students who show stagnation or negative growth. A tiered approach to interventions and support becomes essential to using evidence to ensure success for every student. A score of minimal growth can be viewed as the following.

- The student's scores reflect major deficiencies and learning gaps that a teacher cannot remedy with a single session or what we call an *information and learning center.*

- The student's scores show a marked decline.

- The teacher strongly encouraged the student to visit the information and learning center, but the student chose not to.

- The student's current progress might put him or her on a trajectory that would result in a failing grade at the end of the semester.

- The student rarely or never scores in the 3 range of the gradation in the learning target, even after retakes.

The last two growth indicators are similar to what they mean in traditional grading. *Failure to grow* is handled just like a regular F grade. *Insufficient evidence* means the teacher cannot make a growth determination. Teachers post these growth indicators weekly and communicate them to parents and students.

Separate Student Behavior From Academic Performance

This is somewhat problematic in evidence-based grading because teachers must report behavior separately from academic grades, meaning there is more pressure on students to perform academically. Adding in a social-emotional component to the gradebook offers stakeholders information correlated to performance data. Without this information, students who are bright but have an attitude problem are not fully captured in the gradebook. Figure 2.6 shows the proficiency scores related to student behavior. A score of 3 is proficient, meaning all behavior meets expectations.

Self-Management			
Student	Week 1	Week 2	Week 3
Mohammad	3	3	3
Sarah	3	2	3
John	3	4	4
Suzie	3	2	1

Figure 2.6: Behavior report.

As we wrap up this chapter, we see how our team recognizes the number of shifts that take place when working with an evidence-based grading model. As any team incubates over a new idea in education, it is important that it challenges the idea and makes it its own—in a way that is best for students and implements the valuable changes necessary for better teaching and learning practices to take hold.

Key Points

Review the following key points from this chapter to ensure that you grasp the content. At this point, the team is exiting the incubation phase and begins to have a number of developing insights about making a change toward evidence-based grading. The team is connecting its own best practices around teaching and learning with the ideals of a more equitable and informative grading model centered on evidence of learning and skill growth.

- Setting clear time periods for evidence collection is critical to successful evidence-based grading.
- Student thinking is as important as student outcomes on assessments.
- The gradebook must align to how students are being taught and how they learn.

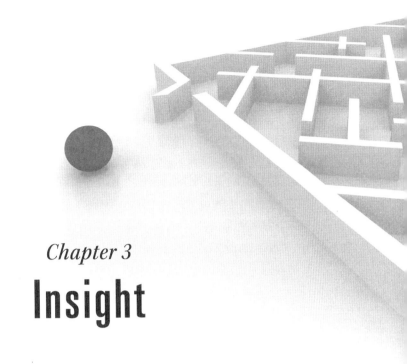

Chapter 3

Insight

At this point in our team's journey, insights start to develop from challenging conversations to generating ideas. When this happens, team members begin to realize more specific values of an evidence-based grading model. They collaboratively discuss their thinking during the preparation and incubation phases, and they make new associations. They recognize the value of the change for ensuring success for every student.

The insight phase is very exciting. This is when the proverbial lightbulb goes on, and we begin to recognize and make important connections—it's the aha moment in the creative process. Team members usually reach these insights at various stages throughout the process. They were developing during the preparation and incubation phases, and will continue to develop during the evaluation and elaboration phases. Sharing and discussing these insights is why collaboration is so important in the creative process.

As you read the team's story, consider how teachers begin to identify insights that help motivate their thoughts about teaching and learning, and note the way these insights contain values directly tied to student growth.

The following are three key points to remember during the insight phase.

1. **Not all insights are positive:** They may be negative or represent obstacles. The key to an insight is that it allows a teacher or a team to use that information to make a change for the better.

2. **Insights usually come from one person:** However, they are likely the culmination of a collaborative team's thoughts and discussions.

3. **Insights need a system of checks and balances:** Good teams review student results to determine if the insight affected learning.

As you read our team's story during the insight phase, pay attention to how insights related to evidence-based grading emerge in the following ways.

- Identify how the team draws valuable connections between the concept of evidence-based grading and its value to student learning.

- Note the way the team thinks about how conversations with students and parents will be more purposeful and specific.

- Find insights that relate to how an evidence-based grading system can better inform instructional efforts.

- Most important, recognize how the team works through the following four shifts: (1) teaching the supporting skills and content up front; (2) having students take on a bigger role in formative assessments and learning target expectations; (3) moving up summative experiences in the pacing of a unit; and (4) placing great value on retakes and reflection.

Our Team's Story

The incubation phase took some time to work through. By this point, Mario and his team have met with small groups of students and parents to explain the concept of evidence-based grading, during which they gathered questions and concerns. They recognize that communicating information about this change is important, and they think if they first work with small groups, they can test out how people understand the idea and gauge any confusion that might emerge.

The team has worked to change its learning targets, create new assessments aligned to those targets, and modify the gradebooks to match the new 4, 3, 2, 1 model of grading.

At the next meeting, Mario asks, "After our small-group discussions with students and families, what are some of the insights that emerged about making the change to an evidence-based grading system?"

While discussing this question, the team reviews the logistics of evidence-based grading, how to communicate a rationale that makes clear sense to students and parents, and the value of evidence-based grading as a way to communicate more clearly about student learning.

Joni begins the conversation. "You know, Mario, moving to evidence-based grading is more of an instructional change than a grading change."

Mario feels that Joni's thinking is the key to more successful teaching and learning. He says, "I think you're right about that, Joni. In order for evidence-based grading to be successful, we need to make some instructional changes. Instructional changes are more than grading changes. A change to evidence-based grading would help our team make more specific and necessary instructional changes."

Britney says, "I'm glad you said that, Mario, because I think the gradebook seems difficult for students to understand, and I'm not sure how it's helping them. I'm a little nervous about the final exams, too."

Mario says that he feels the same way. Then he adds, "The more I work through this change, the more I see it as an instructional change and *not* a grading change. While yes, we have changed our gradebook and we are now giving a 4, 3, 2, 1 score, this is still not what makes evidence-based grading effective. Making and committing to instructional changes are essential to changing our grading system."

"Wait, you need to explain that insight," Kevin says. "How does that make sense? Change instruction to change grading? Those are separate issues, aren't they?"

The others agree with Kevin. Mario says, "In the typical time line, teachers assess frequently; however, it is isolated from instruction—simply verifying learning. In the instructional time line, the unit now includes formatives and retakes; however, the summative experience is still too late in the process. In the evidence-based grading model, the summative experience is further up in the pacing and allows students to understand who they are as learners sooner in the learning process."

The group sits silently, contemplating the new time line.

After a few moments, Britney speaks up. "So what you are saying, Mario, is that we test after one day?"

Kevin interjects, "I think the idea is that we test earlier in the scope and sequence instead of waiting too long to find out how students are learning."

"OK, I know this is my second year of teaching," says Maya, "but what does that mean?"

Mario answers, "Simply put, it means that students learn more effectively in a competency-driven environment; it is essential that they are continually analyzing their current state of understanding of a topic or skill. When they are actively involved in this process, they know where they need to make improvements. This means that they must assess their own learning early and often. They can't find out at the end of the unit that they didn't process or understand the material. Students reflect on their developing proficiency."

"But we give them a chance to understand it," Joni says. "We give them activities, formative assessments, writing, and other activities. What more do we need to do? We have researched all these activities, and we are proud of our work."

Mario says, "Kevin and Joni are right. On one level, our work is really well organized and effective. We do a very good job with our teaching practices. For example, let's say our performance event at the end of unit three is an oral speech about Gettysburg and at no point during our two-week unit did we ask students to orally produce the content. Those are my concerns. At no point prior to our final project did we give students an opportunity to develop their ability to produce an effective oral narrative about historical content. At the end of the unit, we were grading on skills we did not teach them."

"So, maybe we should each discuss Gettysburg with a partner as our warm-up on the second or third day?" Maya asks.

"Yes, exactly! This means that we must give students early opportunities to understand their skills in relation to a specific competency," Mario says.

Kevin asks, "Well, what if you have more than one target per unit?"

"Remember, our work with targets has led us to understand that we don't have many targets anymore. And when we do have multiple targets, we will do the same thing. We need to pay close attention to our students' current state of understanding. The earlier we recognize a student's proficiency level, the earlier we can build improvement."

Joni says, "So our target this unit would be to produce an effective oral narrative with accurate details outlined in class resources. What you are saying, Mario, is that a good portion of our lesson must include the opportunity for students to attempt oral narratives and subsequently reflect on if they were effective and had accurate details from class?"

"Yes, what we need to look at is our pacing. We need to decide what is instructionally important and how we provide experiences for students to make sense of their own learning around the expectations of the target," says Mario.

The team agrees to explore unit three. When it does, it discovers that the unit is in fact disjointed, and the instruction does not align to the target.

Mario says, "Our unit is producing way too much evidence that isn't usable for determining a student's competency."

As the team works to align its instruction, it begins to see many insights into how it can change its instructional approach and provide early opportunities for students to develop the skills they need to succeed.

After a week, the team begins to polish up a few units of study with the early summative judgment pacing structure, and team members are much happier with their new template. Mario then moves to a new area of thought in the meeting, addressing the question that shows up on the team agenda.

"We have a question here about how to score and grade assessments in evidence-based grading," Mario says.

Joni and Maya exchange glances. "Yes, Maya and I just aren't sure if we are grading our assessments correctly," Joni says. "It seems to me that we are simply just giving a 4, 3, 2, or 1 instead of points. It is basically the same thing except for what we write at the top of the paper, right?"

"Well, the way I understand it," Mario says, "evidence-based scoring and evidence-based grading are two different actions. *Scoring* is the act of reviewing the assessment for large- and small-scale patterns in the student's work, and *grading* is providing feedback through conversations with the student based on where he or she fell on the proficiency scale.

"Evidence-based scoring is about pattern recognition. This means that as soon as the teacher sees a pattern of competency or incompetency in a student's work, the teacher comments on it and stops scoring! Yes, stops scoring."

Britney asks, "How can that be?"

Mario responds, "Since the assessments align to the targets correctly as soon as we observe a pattern of work, there is simply no need to continue. But the teacher must start giving feedback. Since there are retakes and growth opportunities, the student can show his or her work again and again. In an evidence-based grading system, scoring and grading are not dependent on each other.

"Traditional grading depends on the teacher adding up all the points earned and dividing those by the total points possible. But in evidence-based grading, scoring is the act of giving feedback about patterns in a student's work, and grading is a conversation about a student's overall proficiency and growth. The teacher can give feedback without an overall ranking and talk about a proficiency ranking before giving any specific feedback. The evidence-based system's flexibility allows for dynamic conversations about growth because participants can move fluidly between both aspects."

"So let me see if I get this," Kevin says. "As soon as I see evidence or a pattern of evidence in a student's work, that gives me insight into the student's proficiency ranking on a target, and I can stop scoring?"

Mario says, "Yes, think about it this way: You know those singing shows on TV? As soon as the judges hear enough, they ask the singer to stop singing, and then the judges provide feedback. Evidence-based grading works the same way. The teacher has an expectation, or target, and as soon as the student provides evidence showing a pattern against or for proficiency, the teacher can move on to a *conversation* with that student. This is the goal of good evidence-based grading—conversations about growth."

The group seems to be getting it. Mario asks that the team calibrates this idea, and it spends the rest of the day working on how to grade and score evidence-based assessments.

The Five Insights in Evidence-Based Grading

During the insight phase of team learning, a team begins to generate exciting revelations into its practices. While the team in our story focuses its efforts on evidence-based grading, it uncovers five very important insights. Teachers must:

1. Use evidence to inform instruction
2. Use evidence to capture current understanding of student proficiency
3. Use evidence for feedback to improve learning (refer to the evidence and explain the need for improvement)
4. Use evidence for scoring
5. Use evidence for grading and reporting

Use Evidence to Inform Instruction

In evidence-based grading, instructional methods must match the *evidence* the learner produces. Simply put, instruction must center on student evidence and highlight how well the students' performance and their own perception of performance (current state) align with expectations (Brown et al., 2014). We think this connection is essential because it solidifies the relationship among curriculum, instruction, and assessment.

Traditional teaching models usually follow this pattern: students view an exemplar, practice the exemplar's components, analyze its elements, and then implement their interpretation of the exemplar for assessment. This is what Peter C. Brown, Henry L. Roediger, and Mark A. McDaniel (2014) call *example learning*.

The two elements of instruction that teachers should consider are structure and execution.

Evidence-Based Lesson Structure

In traditional settings, we find that learning follows a linear, sequential path. This path can hinder students from reaching their true potential. In this linear model, we teach, assess, reflect, and teach again. This continues for the duration of a unit, semester, or year. A linear lesson plan looks something like figure 3.1.

Source: Gobble et al., 2016.

Figure 3.1: Linear lesson plan.

While this is an efficient way to teach, it can foster *shallow learning*—learning cycled through short-term memory only—leaving students feeling like they must cram in more and more knowledge for a quick turnaround.

The evidence-based lesson structure looks much different. Instead, it is a back-and-forth process in which teachers and students produce evidence, react to that evidence through self-assessment and reflection, and produce new evidence to react to. The teacher ensures that there are adequate performance and reflection opportunities within his or her instruction for students to follow this process properly. Figure 3.2 shows how this evidence-based instructional process works.

Produce Evidence   Self-Assess and Reflect

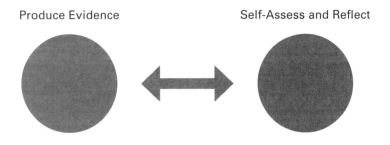

Figure 3.2: Evidence-based lesson plan.

The evidence-based lesson plan places students at the center of learning and creates a nonlinear, dynamically evolving environment in which assessment and instruction act as one rather than separate entities. This combination allows for opportunities to transfer knowledge to new contexts and problems that emerge from interacting with evidence (Brown et al., 2014).

This nimble and flexible structure means teachers can use instruction not just to deliver learning but to actually create it. This reactive practice of instruction is the core of evidence-based grading.

Evidence-Based Lesson Execution

The structure of an evidence-based lesson should include long periods of self-assessment and reflection interwoven with brief periods of performance and feedback. Weaving these experiences together allows a teacher to apply his or her instruction in a dynamic and fluid way. But how does the teacher do this effectively?

Evidence-based instruction challenges teachers and administrators to change their instruction beginning with its smallest component—the learning target. Charlotte Danielson (2007) states that the teacher must convey high expectations for learning to all students and insist on hard work. When teachers focus instruction on proficiency-based learning targets, students are more likely to achieve the intended level of mastery (Gobble et al., 2016).

Brown et al. (2014) state that for learning to be durable and long-lasting, we must connect the content to a diverse set of cues that help students recall the information later. These cues are learning targets. There are four ways teachers can use targets as cues in their instructional practice.

1. **Relate all evidence to the target language:** Teachers should connect what a student says or does to the target's proficiency expectation at every opportunity, giving the target more purpose. An observer should be able to guess the learning target simply by listening to the dialogue in the classroom.

   o An example would be when a teacher walks around the classroom viewing student work and says, "I like what you are doing here with (*language of the target*)" or "I see what you are trying to do here, so make sure (*language of the target*) is more evident."

   o Another example comes from a world language classroom. The learning target is *I can create original oral meaning that is clear and organized and elaborates with supporting details in a simple context.* The teacher might make this target come alive by saying, "I'm not sure what you're trying to say here; remember, clarity is important" or "Your thoughts are detailed, but I suggest that you speak about (*a detail*) before (*a detail*) in order to make more sense."

2. **Explain how tasks for the lesson collect evidence for the target:** Once the teacher outlines the day's tasks, he or she can explain how these relate to the targeted expectation.

   o For example, the teacher might say, "Our tasks today are all connected to (*language of the target*)" or "What I am looking for in regard to (*language of the target*) is . . ."

   o For example, the teacher might say, "Use this moment to discuss how (*language of the target*) can be better displayed in your partners' work."

3. **Capitalize on evidence of student thinking related to the target:** Teachers are responsible for extracting, scrutinizing, and exposing student thinking and reactions related to the target.

- For example, anytime a student or class offers content that relates to the target, the teacher must grab it and teach with it. He or she might say, "That's right, Mia. That information is what we are looking for here in (*language of the target*)" or "What that group just presented is what we mean by (*language of the target*)."

- For example, using the target *I can create original oral meaning that is clear and organized and elaborates with supporting details in a simple context*, the teacher might say, "That is one of the major ways to elaborate with details, Kim" or "Class, let me highlight something Erin just said. She said that originality can be expressed in speaking by (*strategy for creating originality in writing*)."

4. **Use evidence for reflection on the target:** This means that students must use the evidence to form a complete and accurate perspective of their own learning status. The importance of reflection is undeniable, and evidence-based classrooms demand that effective reflection involves quality targets.

- For example, a teacher might ask students the following to prompt them to reflect on learning: "Can you see your work in (*language of the target*) yet?" or "What thinking might go into (*language of the target*)?"

- For example, using the target *I can create original oral meaning that is clear and organized and elaborates with supporting details in a simple context,* the teacher might ask, "Jose, are you certain all your details elaborate on the context of school sports?" or "Remember, class, look at your dialogue. Does it flow logically from one detail to the next about school sports?"

When students work with content in conjunction with proficiency-based learning targets, learning is much more meaningful. Knowledge, skills, and experience that are vivid and hold significance stay in our memories and last forever (Brown et al., 2014).

Use Evidence to Capture Current Understanding of Student Proficiency

All educators know that student engagement increases the impact of learning. However, the problem remains that most students only engage with the material teachers present to them instead of engaging with their own current thinking or learning about the material. While interacting with material develops skill or content knowledge, it does not necessarily establish skills, such as self-efficacy, that help students discern whether their learning is coming together in a competent way. In many classrooms, students never get the opportunity to become highly aware of *where they are* in relation to *what is desirable* (Brown et al., 2014). In evidence-based grading, we refer to this as *current state awareness*, the ability to identify the gap between one's current state and a desired state (Wiliam, 2011). This awareness is critical to growth and learning.

To create this awareness, a teacher must ask him- or herself when students see and engage with their current state of understanding. The main goal of evidence-based instruction is to get students to interact with their current state as much as possible. In order to do that, they must be aware of it.

Aside from knowing how to deploy current state instruction, a teacher must be able to capture a current state when it emerges. While there are many ways to *capture* current states of learning during instruction, we would like to highlight a few we know to be effective.

No-Outcome Assessments

By creating assessment processes that invite students to demonstrate thinking instead of outcomes, teachers can provide the opportunity to reveal their current patterns of thought, pathways of knowledge, and logic used to solve problems. This is called creating *no-outcome assessments*. No-outcome assessments attempt to answer the following question: To what extent are students seeing their own thinking as they engage with problems?

In no-outcome assessments, students must record their approach to solving problems instead of the problems' outcome. Showing their work is not enough. Teachers must present reflective questions, such as, What did you notice about this problem? or What would you add to this scenario? As a comparison, figure 3.3 shows an economics assessment set up in the traditional manner.

---

1. List the four factors of production, and give an example of each.

2. What concept did the shortage simulation illustrate? Explain.

3. Which of the following is real capital?

    a. A share of Apple stock

    b. A savings bond

    c. A truck

    d. A bank account

Figure 3.3: Traditional example of an economics assessment.

Now, let's look at figure 3.4, which shows an economics assessment set up with an opportunity for reflection.

1. Rank the four factors of production (land, labor, entrepreneurship, capital) in order of their importance in an economy. Provide a short explanation for your ranking.

2. The shortage simulation illustrates the concept of scarcity and resource allocation. Please provide another situation that illustrates this concept.

3. If I told you that a share of Apple stock is real capital, would you agree? Explain why or why not.

Figure 3.4: Evidence-based example of an economics assessment.

No-outcome assessments eliminate the need for *classification*, meaning they don't show students the answers. Instead, they engage students with feedback and thinking. This allows students to become aware of their skill development in relation to expectations; it also helps familiarize them with the evidence they need to demonstrate learning growth.

Almost-There Assessments

Another way to do this is to use Myron Dueck's (2014) idea of "I know I am close" (p. 140). This type of assessment asks students to narrow their choices to a few and then explain why each choice could be right. The teacher grades the reasoning, not the outcome, as shown in figure 3.5.

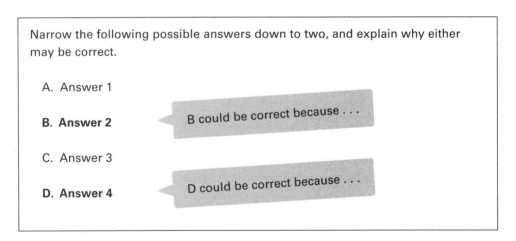

Narrow the following possible answers down to two, and explain why either may be correct.

A. Answer 1

B. Answer 2   B could be correct because . . .

C. Answer 3

D. Answer 4   D could be correct because . . .

Figure 3.5: Almost-there assessment.

Almost-there assessments allow a teacher to examine each student's current state of thinking or performance against different perspectives. No-outcome assessments allow for perspective verification, mental mapping of development and growth, and solidified learning.

Formative Realization

Even though teachers may view themselves as portals to learning, in evidence-based grading, they are not access points. Rather, a teacher is more like a learning conscience, pushing students to create new learning and make connections while holding them to fidelity in the desired proficiency or skill. In other words, the teacher's primary responsibility is to ensure that all students are engaging reflectively with a proficiency-based target.

This means that teachers must focus their instruction primarily on providing opportunities for *formative realization*, instead of *formative verification*. Students should use assessment to become highly aware of where their performance and thinking are taking them in their learning. When teachers allow learners to engage with assessments, such as no-outcome assessments, for long and uninterrupted periods of time, students can start to consider how to learn the material in a more flexible manner. This is important because learning is about making connections with new ideas and examining those connections as often as possible. Students in an evidence-based environment need time to make connections, and we must give it to them.

Cognitive Engagement

With so much research focusing on active classroom engagement, many teachers don't pay attention to the level of cognitive engagement students exhibit throughout a lesson. We define *cognitive engagement* as the time students spend reflectively engaging with their current state of learning. Throughout a traditional lesson, cognitive engagement swells and drops often, sometimes unpredictably. Traditionally minded teachers have a tendency to interpret engagement through the lens of physical engagement first, asking for actions such as "Talk with your shoulder partner about . . . ," "Work with the group to make . . . ," or "Discuss with your group . . . ." These are all important and necessary; however, simply engaging students in physical activity with content only goes so far. In evidence-based grading, teachers build the intensity of cognitive engagement throughout the lesson.

A teacher who focuses on the targeted proficiency pays more attention to cognitive engagement. For example, Danielson (2007) states that students invite comments from their classmates during a discussion. The important word here is *invite*. Inviting doesn't mean simply sharing comments with peers because the teacher says so. Inviting someone to make a comment relies on a particular student's ability to understand his or her current state of learning enough to consciously *know* what to ask of others. If students are not aware of their current state of learning, they simply won't be able to ask cognitively stimulating and challenging questions. In fact, in our observations, without this cognitive engagement, students simply engage in repetitive discussion of the formulaic steps that satisfy the task for the task's sake.

For example, in mathematics, students without cognitive engagement may have a discussion such as, "First, you add this to that, and then you divide by . . ." Or, in English, it might sound like, "In the first paragraph, you need five sentences that have a main point, like the one the teacher provided."

This might be engagement, but it is not cognitive engagement. Engagement without cognitive thinking is simply mimicry, with no need to clarify thinking or to ask someone what he or she thinks—just satisfy the task at hand. Mimicry simply keeps students busy copying the exemplar or satisfying what the model rubric outlines without any current state awareness. In an evidence-based classroom, where there is minimal mimicry, students focus on figuring out how well they are doing, exploring the target they must achieve, and maintaining the level of mastery the teacher expects.

Danielson (2013) emphasizes the value of collaborative, student-to-student interactions within her framework for teacher evaluation. Students review each other's work, problem solve, and help one another learn. Danielson (2013) wants to see classrooms where "a student asks another student if anyone else knows how to figure [something] out" (p. 55). Students seeking interaction with other students can happen in more authentic ways because they are highly aware of their current state of learning.

By keeping students focused on their current state of learning, we can inspire them to engage more cognitively. Table 3.1 compares questions that invite mimicry to those that invite cognitive engagement.

Table 3.1: Mimicry Versus Cognitive Engagement

Questions That Invite Mimicry	Questions That Invite Cognitive Engagement
"What do you think about this topic?"	"If I told you (a fact, information, context), what would you think?"
"What three ways can you answer this question?"	"What if I changed (a fact, information, context)? Would you still feel or think the same way?"
"How can you answer this question, including all the essential details?"	"By adding (a detail), would you change your mind?"

wondering? reading?

The cognitive questions, which evidence-based grading uses often, keep students engaged with their current state of understanding, while the mimicry questions invite a formulaic or even robotic response.

Our observation of non–evidence-based classrooms reveals that students' cognitive engagement rose and fell during the lesson. In many lessons that we have observed, the teacher told students something to the effect of "Here are the directions on what to do; now go do them and make it look like this." In many observations over the years, we have seen cognitive engagement act erratically, as shown in figure 3.6.

For each observation in which we focused on cognitive engagement, we charted the time students spent actively reflecting on a learning target as well as each time cognitive engagement rose and fell dramatically.

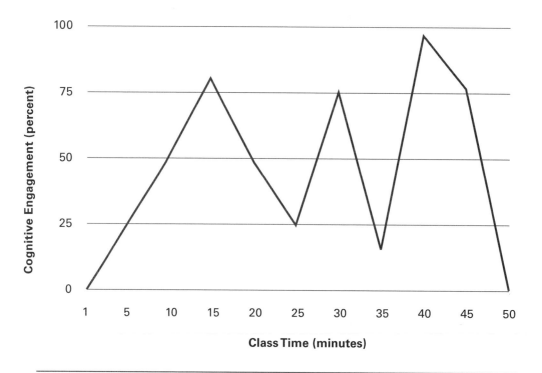

Figure 3.6: Inconsistent cognitive engagement.

In evidence-based grading, teachers consider cognitive engagement more crucial than mimicry, and it is always on the rise. In our observations of evidence-based courses, cognitive engagement looks like the chart in figure 3.7.

Cognitive engagement is the best resource for discovering one's current state of learning. Danielson (2013) states, "The pacing of the lesson provides students the time needed not only to intellectually engage with and reflect upon their learning

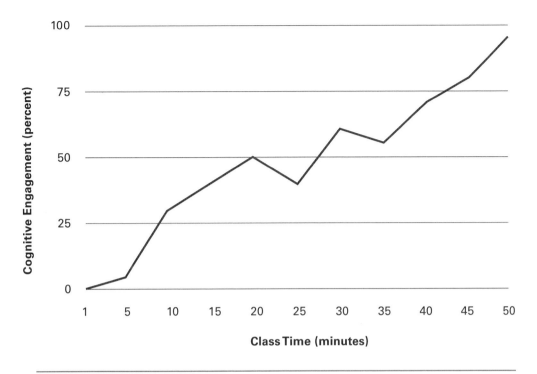

Figure 3.7: Consistently increasing cognitive engagement.

but also to consolidate their understanding" (p. 51). To some teachers, this statement might mean that students should write down what they learned in an exit slip or reflective journaling activity at the end of class. However, in evidence-based grading, this means what Danielson (2007) intends it to mean: being cognitively engaged with one's own current state of learning in dynamically authentic areas *throughout* the lesson. In evidence-based instruction, we strive not to have students *prove* their learning but rather to have them *engage* with it.

Use Evidence for Feedback to Improve Learning

Giving students feedback is a relatively straightforward process. Teachers assess student work and tell them how to improve. However, getting students to actually *interact* with feedback can be difficult. It is crucial to success. There are several effective ways to get students to interact with feedback more successfully and meaningfully (Adair-Hauck, Glisan, & Troyan, 2013), such as evidence-based rubrics and co-constructed feedback.

Evidence-Based Rubrics

Rubrics are one of the main portals through which students view feedback in an evidence-based grading course. We believe rubrics can be ineffective if not used appropriately. As Reeves (2016a, 2016b) claims, rubrics must not ask only for mimicry of criteria. Unfortunately, many rubrics do just this by outlining the *specific* criteria students must include in their work to earn points. The teacher determines how a student performed by accumulating and totaling those points. This doesn't work in an evidence-based system.

Rubrics in an evidence-based classroom first and foremost rank student performance in one overall judgment—how the student did—not simply by what the student included or didn't include in the performance. This means that a rubric's most important role is to classify a student and then separately yet simultaneously communicate the list of criteria that led to that classification. Most rubrics act as either a communicator of every single possible criteria or a classifier of everything.

This idea is similar to learning to drive a car. Some people remember this experience as very frustrating. This may be because whoever taught them was most likely attempting to classify them and communicate with them at the same time. The driving teacher may have sounded something like this: "OK, now ease your foot off the brake; now slowly turn the wheel to the right a bit but *not too far.* OK, now straighten out . . . *but don't step on the brake too much.* All right now, that's it. Keep your hands on the wheel. OK, you are doing fine. Check your mirrors. Now give it a little gas . . . more gas . . . no more gas. *Please step on the brake!* What are you doing? We are going home!"

You may laugh as you read this, but this is what rubrics are doing to our students! Students can't help but feel confused when classification and communication occupy the same cognitive and feedback space. Students may be asking, "Where is the feedback? What is a judgment? How did I do exactly?"

With evidence-based rubrics, teachers first classify and then move to communicate. To test to see if your rubrics are communicating and classifying accurately, ask yourself, "Can a learner clearly identify which area is classification and which area is communication?" Let's take a look at an example of a rubric that you don't want to use—one that classifies and communicates at the same time. See figure 3.8.

This kind of rubric can be dangerous because there are too many assumptions and no criteria listed—the learner might not know where his or her ranking or feedback is. This rubric tries to serve two purposes (classification and communication) simultaneously and provides too much information. There are far too many classification scales, so it is hard for the learner to figure out what is important or how to improve.

Speaking Rubric				
Criteria	**High** **(5–6)**	**Mid–High** **(3–4)**	**Mid–Low** **(2)**	**Low** **(1)**
Content: Content and details	Student provides many rich and detailed examples.	Student provides many meaningful examples.	Student provides some appropriate examples.	Student provides a few vague examples.
Engagement: Attention, active listening, responsiveness	Student's remarks capture and hold the listener's attention; always uses active listening strategies.	Student's remarks capture the listener's attention; uses active listening strategies the majority of the time.	Student's remarks attempt to engage the listener; sometimes uses active listening strategies.	Student's remarks do not engage the listener; rarely uses active listening strategies.
Vocabulary: All vocabulary from unit, five words from each list	Student uses accurate and advanced vocabulary and concepts.	Student uses accurate and appropriate vocabulary and concepts.	Student uses vocabulary and concepts with some accuracy.	Student uses vocabulary and concepts with minimal to no accuracy.

Score: 30 + _____ = _____ / 60

55–60 = A   45–54 = B   35–44 = C   30–34 = D   0–29 = F

Figure 3.8: Non-evidence-based grading rubric that classifies and communicates.

A student receiving this rubric might think, "Is the teacher ranking *everything* I did?" or "Where are the criteria used to give me that ranking?" or "How can I be a *novice* in one area but an *expert* in another connected to the same skill? How can I be high in a lot of areas and get a B from total points?" To help clarify this point, we look to O'Connor (2009), who states that it is important to distinguish between *feedback* and *guidance*: "Feedback provides descriptive information about what the student did, while guidance provides information about what the student should do to improve" (p. 125).

Wiggins (1998) builds on this idea:

> We take this same principle and apply it to successful rubric creating and deployment, where the feedback [classification] must act in a holistic manner, yielding a single score based on an overall impression. Then move to a communication [guidance stance] that isolates each trait or criteria to show how to improve. (as cited in Reeves, 2016a, p. 24)

The balance between classification (feedback about performance) and communication (guidance about how to get better) is delicate. With perhaps too much classification and too little communication, a student might see the rubric as a static ranking instead of a formative opportunity. On the other hand, a heavily communication-based rubric might promote mimicry.

The result from either of these scenarios is that students may not view the feedback or evidence from their work as transformational for learning. They might see it more as *what they were* instead of *who they can become.*

Evidence-based rubrics must contain three components in order to balance feedback properly.

1. **Proficiency-based targets:** Make sure to create proficiency-based targets—targets that holistically rank student performance or knowledge level.

2. **Criteria for success and supporting content:** Clearly identify criteria for success, prerequisite skills, and knowledge required for successful attainment of the target's proficiency levels.

3. **A conversation sandbox:** Build a conversation sandbox—a feedback space for the teacher and student to have a conversation about performance and its interplay with the criteria.

Let's examine how a rubric like figure 3.9 includes these three components to promote learning dialogues and reflection. (Visit **go.SolutionTree.com /assessment** to download a free reproducible version of this figure.)

Figure 3.10 (page 90) shows an example of a completed evidence-based rubric for a proficiency-based learning target for speaking.

Evidence-based rubrics are an essential vehicle for interacting with students and getting them to interact with the evidence they produce. If used correctly, evidence-based rubrics can provide fertile ground to grow co-constructed learning environments. Without evidence-based rubrics, the assessment process cannot become an active element of grading, as we explain in the next section.

Learning Target	Level 4 Extends	Level 3 Meets	Level 2 Approaches	Level 1 Basic
Unscaled Criteria	**Conversation Sandbox**		**Conversation Sandbox**	
Criterion One				
Criterion Two				
Criterion Three				
Criterion Four				
Unscaled Supporting Content and Skills				
Supporting Skill One				
Supporting Skill Two				
Supporting Skill Three				
Supporting Skill Four				

Figure 3.9: Example of an evidence-based rubric.

Learning Target	4	3	2	1
Independently create an appropriate spoken message in familiar and unstructured situations.	Independently create an appropriate spoken message in unfamiliar and unstructured situations.	Independently create an appropriate spoken message in familiar and unstructured situations.	Independently create an appropriate spoken message in familiar and structured situations.	Independently attempt to create an appropriate spoken message in familiar and structured situations.

Communication Strategies	Student Reflection	Teacher Feedback
Engagement	I used good vocabulary and details.	*Your vocabulary was good; however, you could have included a few more stretch words and terms that were on your vocabulary worksheet. Also, I am hoping that you include more than basic details in your speech. If you read the homework each night, you will gain confidence in your speaking because you can use more details. This will help you improve your body language and delivery.*
Delivery	I was a little nervous, which could be why I didn't have the best eye contact and delivery.	
Risk Taking		
Body Language	I forgot to add in the content piece we talked about during the formative practice speech.	
Supporting Skills		
Vocabulary		
Context Details		
Connections		
Evidence		

Figure 3.10: Example of a completed evidence-based rubric.

Co-Constructed Feedback

There should be no surprises in evidence-based grading because feedback is quick, and often, data are simply more accessible to the student. Students feel much more connected to learning than with traditional methods. When feedback is timely, students are not surprised by it. When feedback is accurate, they experience no expectation gap. The *expectation gap* is the gap between what students think the teacher wants and what the teacher actually wants. Teachers and students should engage in a co-constructed feedback process to mitigate this situation.

Co-constructed feedback is a process the American Council on the Teaching of Foreign Languages practitioners developed and used in many world language classrooms. Teachers can achieve co-construction by asking students to give themselves feedback before their teacher gives them feedback. This may seem ineffective or even impossible, but as Brown et al. (2014) write:

> As you cast about for a solution, retrieving related knowledge from memory, you strengthen the route to a gap in your learning even before the answer is provided to fill it and, when you do fill it, connections are made to the related material. . . . Unsuccessful attempts to solve a problem encourage deep processing of the answer when it is later supplied, creating fertile ground for its encoding. (p. 88)

When students have time to give themselves feedback and the teacher verifies or reinforces that feedback, they can begin to trust their own thinking. This is what we emphasize throughout this book, and it is essential to quality learning. Here's what this process would look like in five steps (Zizzo, 2015).

1. Students perform (any event) to produce evidence.

2. Students review their evidence alone or in pairs using reflection guides or evidence-based rubrics.

3. Students meet with the teacher, individually or in pairs, to review the evidence. Students do all the talking as they present evidence in conjunction with their self-evaluation.

4. The teacher interprets what students presented.

5. Students and the teacher agree on a proficiency rating, and the feedback generated connects to growth and future learning.

The main idea with co-constructed feedback is that the teacher is not the first and only person to evaluate evidence. The first eyes on a student's completed work should always be the student's. If students review and evaluate their work first and *then* corroborate their findings with the teacher, they can generate a more accurate picture of their current state of learning.

Use Evidence for Scoring

Scoring evidence-based assessments is much different from scoring points-based assessments. The goal of scoring evidence-based assessments is to provide feedback, not tally up what is right or wrong within the work. Teachers should concentrate on two objectives to achieve this goal: (1) start with feedback and (2) recognize learning patterns.

Start With Feedback

Teachers often move too quickly to classify students (give them a grade) and then provide feedback after the fact. Instead, teachers must *pause* the classification of student work and give feedback first. Brown et al. (2014) state that "delaying the feedback [classification] briefly produces better long-term learning than immediate feedback [classification]" (p. 39). Assessment has become a tighter interaction of grading and feedback, but immediate rankings are not always good for students.

Simply asking the student to think about the feedback first allows learning the space it needs to become more entrenched. When a student finishes an assessment, the teacher can provide feedback about what he or she sees in the work without judging it. This simple act infuses mindfulness into the scoring process. Figure 3.11 shows how this might look for an evidence-based assessment.

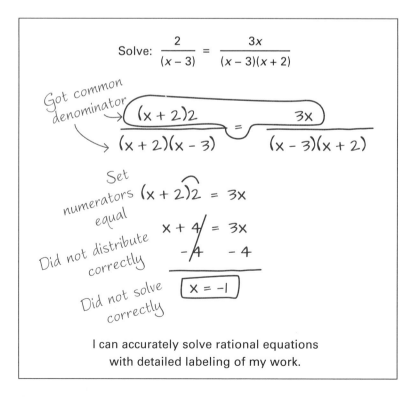

Figure 3.11: Evidence-based feedback used in scoring.

In traditional scoring, on the other hand, feedback comes *after* the scoring, so scoring would look more like figure 3.12.

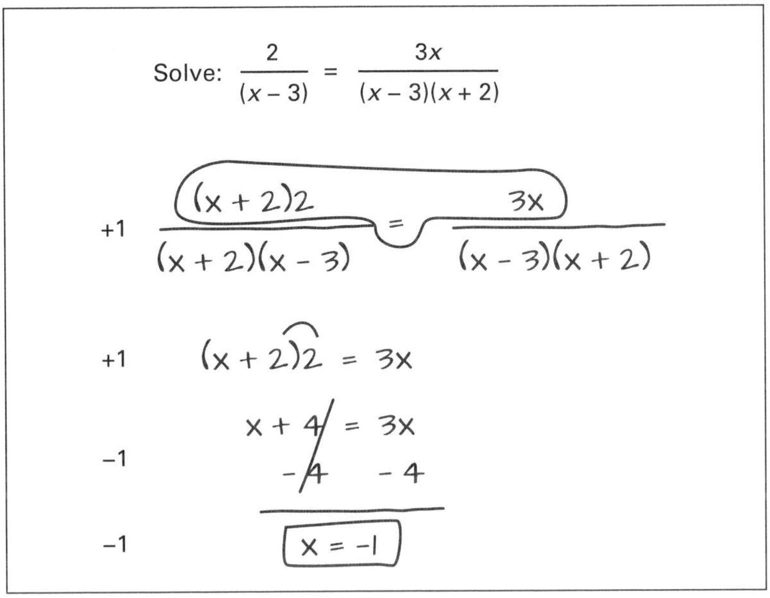

$$\text{Solve:} \quad \frac{2}{(x-3)} = \frac{3x}{(x-3)(x+2)}$$

$$+1 \qquad \frac{(x+2)2}{(x+2)(x-3)} = \frac{3x}{(x-3)(x+2)}$$

$$+1 \qquad (x+2)2 = 3x$$

$$-1 \qquad x + 4 = 3x$$
$$\qquad\qquad -4 \qquad -4$$

$$-1 \qquad \boxed{x = -1}$$

Figure 3.12: Traditional scoring.

While feedback first may seem a bit odd, it is a very effective way to score assessments and essential to evidence-based scoring. Delaying judgment gives students a properly paced formative cycle that allows them to develop a heightened focus on their own work (Brown et al., 2014).

Recognize Learning Patterns

Evidence-based scoring is about finding learning patterns in the evidence. As soon as a teacher sees a pattern, he or she gives feedback about that pattern. As Mario states in our team's story, it is like judging a singing audition. As soon as the judge sees patterns of evidence that support or disprove the proficiency outlined in the learning target (what the judge is looking for), he or she stops the performance and provides feedback about which patterns are small and which are large. *Small* means minor issues, and *large* means major roadblocks to proficiency. The point is that the judge doesn't need to listen to the entire performance; he or she stops the performance once he or she has identified patterns of evidence and then moves quickly to feedback and conversations.

This is the same concept underlying evidence-based scoring; the goal is to recognize patterns. As soon as we see those patterns, we stop scoring and give more feedback. Figure 3.13 (page 94) shows how this looks in evidence-based assessment.

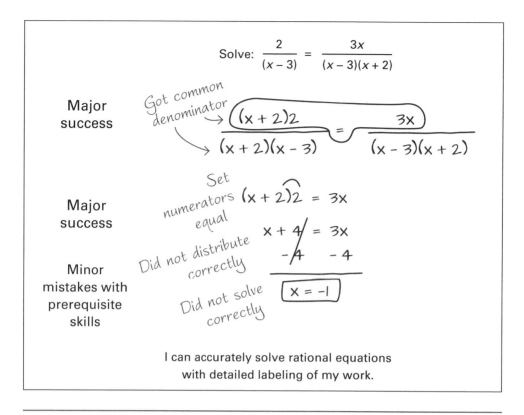

Figure 3.13: Example of pattern recognition in evidence-based scoring.

Notice in this example the teacher adds another layer to the feedback, citing major and minor proficiency patterns in the evidence. There are no points or marks on the assessment, just words that invite conversations and provide context for learning.

With evidence-based scoring, feedback is the grade. Teachers must give it often, freely, and honestly. Without pattern recognition and feedback, teachers struggle to score evidence-based assessments.

Use Evidence for Grading and Reporting

As teachers make use of evidence for the purposes of grading, they must consider how they package and state feedback in a way that is going to communicate clearly to a student about his or her performance and development.

Packaging Feedback

If evidence-based scoring is about giving feedback, then evidence-based grading is about how we *package* that feedback. Traditional grading typically packages feedback with an overall total of points earned out of points possible, as shown in figure 3.14.

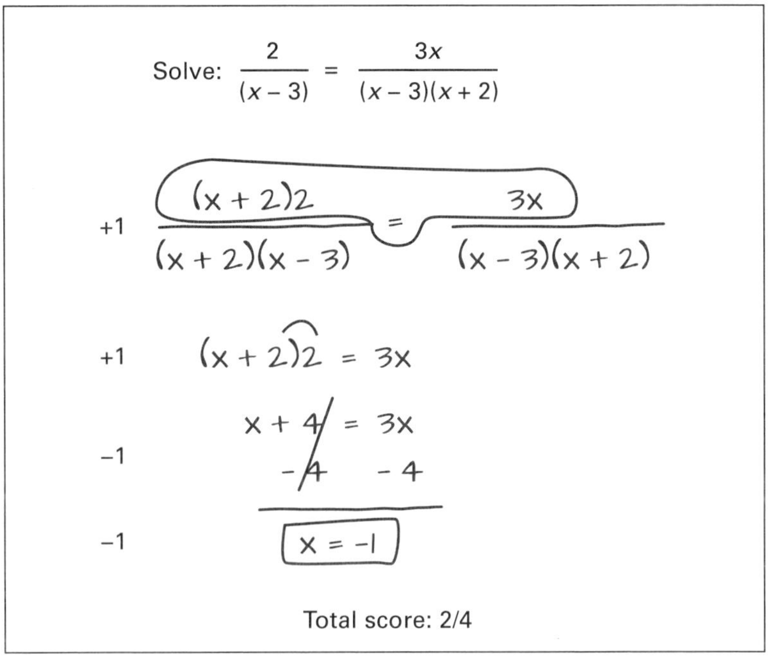

$$\text{Solve:} \quad \frac{2}{(x-3)} = \frac{3x}{(x-3)(x+2)}$$

+1 $\frac{(x+2)2}{(x+2)(x-3)} = \frac{3x}{(x-3)(x+2)}$

+1 $(x+2)2 = 3x$

−1 $x + 4 = 3x$
$ - 4 \quad - 4$

−1 $\boxed{x = -1}$

Total score: 2/4

Figure 3.14: Example of packaging feedback in traditional grading.

Packaging feedback in this way typically leaves students confused, deflated, overconfident, indignant, or a whole host of other reactions due to the muddled nature of the grade. Students are left to rationalize helplessly, "What is 2/4? Does it really represent who I am? Can I recover from this? What went wrong? What went right?"

In evidence-based grading, feedback packaging is much different. A proficiency-based target packages the feedback from scoring evidence-based assessments, since there are no points. The teacher simply communicates to students the proficiency level he or she suggests that relates to the skill or content he or she is assessing. Figure 3.15 (page 96) shows an example of how this might look.

Communicating About Evidence-Based Grades

Evidence-based grading revolves around *conversations*, not just classifying and categorizing performance. Grading focuses on helping students move to the next level of proficiency instead of stating why they did not earn enough points to be considered proficient.

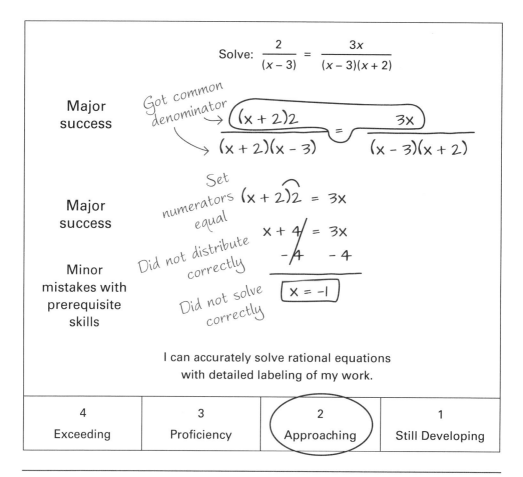

Figure 3.15: Example of packaging feedback in evidence-based grading.

These conversations are about the patterns of proficiency students display when teachers score their work and how those patterns relate to the proficiency teachers expect when they outline learning targets. Teachers must review, scrutinize, and co-construct evidence into new learning; it's a challenge. But as a result, students are more focused on learning, not the grade. One mathematics student put it this way: "In evidence-based grading, you know you really know the material, or you *really* see that you don't."

When having evidence-based grading conversations with students, teachers should consider the following three key ideas.

1. **Evidence-based grading conversations must be *mutual*:** Purposeful co-construction of learning is born in the absence of points and percentages. The teacher and students interact with kinship instead of autocracy. Mutual trust in the evidence fosters a meaningful grading

relationship between teacher and students, in which both parties trust that the feedback is accurate.

2. **Evidence-based grading conversations must be *prescriptive*:** Prescriptive conversations are focused on growth and progress. In these conversations, participants analyze the evidence and discuss how it can cause new learning to blossom or solidify. The teacher might say something like, "This skill will lead you to being able to . . ." Grading is less reactive than with traditional methods. When conversations are reactive, they tend to be more negative, based on what went wrong. They act as a remediation tool, even when the teacher uses positive language. For example, the teacher might say, "Fix the gaps in your work, and then you will get it."

3. **Evidence-based grading conversations must be *rewarding*:** Evidence-based grading conversations must engender the perspective in every student that he or she can succeed. As noted earlier, students should focus on learning, not getting a grade. For example, a student in an evidence-based course might say, "I have a chance to learn, recover from mistakes, and ultimately succeed."

In figure 3.15, notice that the student's score is *approaching mastery*. This student receives specific feedback on major proficiency patterns in his or her work. The message to this student is positive, specific, and actionable.

Key Points

Now, take the time to review the following key points from this chapter to ensure that you grasp the content. As you work with your team, remember that each person's insights are important to how to implement and use an evidence-based grading model effectively. The insight phase helps educators locate smarter connections to how students demonstrate evidence of learning and how we create dialogues around learning.

- The teacher and student must discuss and validate feedback together.
- Rubrics must contain three components: (1) proficiency-based targets, (2) criteria for success and supporting content, and (3) a conversation sandbox.
- Evidence-based grading is based on conversations about evidence of learning and skills; it is not based on conversations about earning points.

Chapter 4

Evaluation

As our team begins to incorporate an evidence-based grading model into its classrooms, reviewing and evaluating its effectiveness and value must be ongoing and immediate. Some teachers on the team will quickly meet with success, while others might struggle to implement the new approach in a way that makes sense. The evaluation phase is meant to identify what is working and what is not working about the shift. Not everything will work perfectly the first time.

When we actually implement a change, we begin to see all sorts of concerns we didn't anticipate. Allowing for ongoing evaluation of a change like this demands attention to team reflection and problem solving. Evaluation's main focus is collaborative support of the full team; teammates must depend on one another for support, input, and candidness.

While you are reading about this phase of our team's journey, pay attention to how and why team members know the implementation is taking hold and whether it is reaching its goal. Remember, implementing an evidence-based grading model increases students' explicit understanding of skill development and how those skills are demonstrated and improved.

For any reflective evaluation, we suggest working through an evaluative protocol so the conversation is focused and valuable for all team members. For instance, the team might decide to do three case studies that objectively examine both positive and negative experiences with implementing evidence-based grading. Sharing might take the form of identifying patterns of concerns and patterns of successes. The outcome might be to create an action plan to address the implementation issues the case studies bring forward and that the team solves. Teams should address concerns quickly and thoughtfully, making sure students and parents are clear about classroom expectations.

Following are three key points to remember during the evaluation phase.

1. Team members should continually evaluate successes and concerns during the implementation process of evidence-based grading.

2. In evidence-based grading, evaluation is different—the data help build more specific discussions around teaching and learning, gaps in learning, and ways to advance learning.

3. During the evaluation phase, teams should listen for how students are talking about learning and redirect conversations that might fall back on points or percentages.

Our Team's Story

As the second half of the year begins, the team is reinvigorated. Team members see the relationships between evidence-based grading and instructional change. Mario and his team have several productive meetings as they revise and try new lesson plans to include more clarity and directedness about evidence-based grading and how they discuss learning with students.

Mario knows it will be important to regularly evaluate and reflect on evidence-based grading's implementation. He and the team agree that this approach will definitely involve them in deeper conversations about their instruction and student learning.

At the first meeting, Britney expresses a concern. "We've been doing evidence-based grading for a while now," she says. "We made mistakes, but I feel like we corrected them. Yet our final exam test scores are lower than they've been in the past. I'm concerned that my students aren't learning as well." Kevin and Maya have the same problem. When they review data, they determine that test scores are not heading in the right direction.

Mario asks if Joni has seen similar results. She responds, "I feel like I am assessing too much, and students are tired of the constant focus on assessment. Personally, I can't keep up with grading, especially if we also consider allowing students to retake assessments. It's all a bit harder than I thought, and I'm having a hard time seeing the benefits."

Mario listens closely before replying. "Thank you for sharing your concerns openly," he says. "That is important for us to continue doing. The central question is always, Is this good for our students? If not, why are we doing it?"

According to a student satisfaction survey, most of Mario's students rate his class three times higher than the other team members' students rate their classes, and most of his students rate their evidence-based grading experience as excellent. Some even say that it transformed their idea of school in a positive way. This survey, along with his experience in the classroom with evidence-based grading, gives Mario the confidence to lead his team through this challenging time.

Mario says, "Before we evaluate our efforts in implementing evidence-based grading, let's start by asking, 'Do we have enough of the right evidence?'"

"What do you mean?" Kevin asks.

"In an evidence-based environment, our students produce so much evidence at any given time that we must take time to review our lessons to see if we have the *right* evidence. Without that, we run the risk of creating a disconnected and overassessed learning environment."

Britney says, "That is exactly what I feel . . . like we are overassessing our students and not teaching all that we need to because of the high number of tests and retakes."

"That is why this question is so important," says Mario. "First, let's decide what we mean by the *right assessments*. We need to determine if our assessments speak the language of the learning targets. In other words, what is the through-line of our assessments?"

Joni asks, "What do you mean by a *through-line*?"

"I mean *how* do our assessments align to the language of our learning targets?" Mario replies.

Kevin removes some assessments from his bag and responds to Mario's original question. "Of course we do. Look here. We are teaching the Cold War, and all these tests capture evidence of matching vocabulary, recognizing key events, writing a thesis paper, and reading articles about historical figures. We have plenty."

The team members agree.

Mario says, "Yes, but our target is *I can effectively produce an oral narrative that sufficiently describes the historical time period.* The key word here is *orally*."

The team is silent for a moment, and then Joni says, "To achieve this learning target, students practice for speaking, read and write about historical events, and engage in activities with vocabulary and facts. In other words, students are doing a number of different learning tasks."

"In a competency-based environment, evidence is produced by *all* these activities," says Mario. "However, these activities don't necessarily help the student develop competency in the targeted objective. Furthermore, we can't use any evidence from reading and writing activities to determine who the learner is in relation to this particular target.

"In an evidence-based environment in which evidence of proficiency determines learning, assessments must capture what the proficiency objective or target demands. These targets derive from a curriculum that the department or school has adopted; in our case, our learning targets come from the Common Core. The evidence of competency must come from assessments that are aligned to the targeted proficiency."

Joni voices a concern. "So, are we just teaching to the test now?"

Mario answers, "No, we are developing a proficiency. We can only develop proficiency with clearly interwoven assessments. We need to approach our work from that mindset. We can vary our assessment structure and interweave other proficiencies as we interpret evidence, but we can never use evidence from an assessment that doesn't relate to the language of the target."

Kevin says, "But our students are learning just fine with all the practice. Why does it have to align? Is this change really good for our students?"

Mario notes that the scheduled end time for the meeting is drawing near and senses that there will not be a resolution at this time. He presses on. "Yes, it is a good change, although we will not immediately see the effects of the change. It is good because all students are doing now is renting knowledge instead of building proficiency. They can only achieve short-term retention because we have no proficiency through-line in our assessments."

Maya chimes in and asks for clarification. "So, what you are saying is that on one of our first days of the unit, even our warm-up should match the proficiency expectation we are asking for on the performance event or exam at the end of the unit?"

Mario, not expecting this answer, smiles emphatically. "Exactly! And your warm-ups also should match the quizzes, projects, and any formative assessments we may have. This is not to say we only have one target per unit. We can interweave many targets throughout a unit and decide which are eligible for interpretation."

A sense of relief strikes the group in the last few minutes of the meeting, so Mario decides to end on a high note. "We must carefully analyze our assessments to make sure they are providing enough evidence of learning. This helps make sure that we are creating assessments around the right proficiencies to make informed decisions about our students. Right now, our instructional scope and sequence of any particular unit is mostly disconnected and relatively unrelated to the learning target."

The team members leave with an action step for moving forward: to examine how they are creating assessments that provide the evidence needed to make better decisions about teaching and learning.

The Six Key Questions in Evidence-Based Grading

During the evaluation phase, teams must focus on how to effectively collaborate on results and data. Teams should build assessment models that allow students to demonstrate the visible evidence of their learning. When evaluating the effectiveness of an evidence-based grading approach, our team must consider the effectiveness of the work: Are students demonstrating proficiency? How well are they reaching and mastering learning goals? What reflections and conversations about learning are taking place, and what does success look and sound like for students?

During the evaluation phase, the collaborative team members must answer six critical questions regarding evidence-based grading.

1. Are we collecting the right evidence to determine a grade?

2. Are we effectively communicating learning targets and standards?

3. Are we providing opportunities for student growth?

4. Are we separating academic and behavior information in the gradebook?

5. Are we ensuring student accountability?

6. Are we creating effective evidence-based gradebooks?

Are We Collecting the Right Evidence to Determine a Grade?

Deciding on the right evidence to determine how we grade, evaluate, and provide feedback to students is an important collaborative discussion for teams. When team members agree on what proficiency or mastery looks or sounds like, they are more calibrated in their judgments. They have come to a common understanding of what expectations not only are appropriate for a certain subject and grade level but will approach grading with greater equity.

The reality is that many schools try to adopt evidence-based grading using their current assessment models. This is an issue because 20th and 21st century assessment models, however refined, still ask for mimicry instead of exposing students' thought construction about learned material (Brown et al., 2014). They simply do not provide good information to help engage students in conversations about learning and growth. Successful implementation of an evidence-based grading model depends on effective assessments that move beyond rewarding mimicry and aim to reveal areas for growth and development (Brown et al., 2014).

Teachers need assessments that lean toward reflective interaction as much as achievement. Evidence-based assessments aim to capture shallow learning that may have occurred. They aim to not only prepare the student's mind for future thinking but also find out what the student is currently thinking (Chappuis, 2009; Marzano, 2006).

Evidence-based assessments gather evidence of emotional reactions, patterns of thinking, and cognitive allusions that occur while a student solves for an outcome. In *Making Thinking Visible: How to Promote Engagement, Understanding, and Independence for All Learners*, Ron Ritchhart, Mark Church, and Karin Morrison (2011) quote a teacher they interview: "I judge my students not by the answers they give, but by the questions they ask" (p. 32). While we acknowledge that not all assessment can work this way, evidence-based grading environments demand this assessment mindset.

Evidence-based assessments attempt to expose mental models, not verify them. A *mental model* is a mental representation of absorbed knowledge (Brown et al., 2014). During the learning process, students absorb ideas from the instruction and construct them into a coherent framework (Brown et al., 2014). The problem is that students don't always create the most effective mental models, so teachers can use evidence-based assessments to expose, analyze, and improve them. The structure of these assessments should include opportunities for reflection and formative practice and ultimately provide a clear picture of who the student is as a learner.

As we previously stated, traditional assessments simply can't capture all that happens as a student engages with learning and performance. In *Make It Stick: The Science of Successful Learning*, Brown et al. (2014) emphasize this idea. "It seems that a significant portion of [students'] working memory capacity is expended monitoring their performance (How am I doing? Am I making mistakes?), leaving less working memory capacity available to solve the problems posed by the test" (Brown et al., 2014, p. 91). We could not agree more.

Evidence-based assessments capture students' reflective thinking and try to document the context in which they arrive at outcomes. Ritchhart et al. (2011) write:

> Documentation of students' thinking serves another important purpose in that it provides a phase from which both teachers and students may observe the learning process, make note of the strategies being used, and comment on the developing understanding. The visibility afforded by documentation provides the basis for reflecting on one's learning and for considering that learning as an object for discussion. (p. 39)

We take this to mean that assessment is a crucial part of reflecting and the catalyst for great feedback. While some teachers see reflection and feedback as activities to do *after* an assessment, we argue that reflection and feedback should be done *throughout* an assessment. For an example of this, we asked Ms. Fenton, a mathematics teacher, to give us a mathematics assessment. See figure 4.1. The exam simply asked students to solve problems. There were four answer choices for each problem, and the exam included minimal context.

Solve. Show all work.

1. $2x^2 + 3x + 1$
   a. -1
   b. $-1/2$
   c. 3
   d. 10

2. $2x^2 + 9x + 4$
   a. 2.12
   b. 3.12
   c. 2.62
   d. 1.41

Figure 4.1: Traditional mathematics assessment.

We took the exam . . . and failed it. We asked the teacher to walk us through it. The teacher's behavior quickly changed, and she began asking us questions. She asked, "What was the first thing you looked at? Where did you have to change the problem?" (C. Fenton, personal communication, October 12, 2013).

This observation is significant because the "voice" of the assessment differed dramatically from what the teacher asked to gauge our understanding of mathematics. The exam asked us for outcomes—to arrive at correct answers. But when the teacher started to gauge our understanding, she based it on our reflective thinking, not our outcomes! At the end of this exercise, we asked her, "Why doesn't the assessment ask the same questions you are asking?" Through our discussion, this teacher realized that combining thinking and outcomes is possible, and she changed her assessment. Figure 4.2 (page 106) shows this new assessment.

Complete the following and show all your work when applicable.

1. Solve: $2x^2 + 3x + 1$.

2. What is the first thing you looked at to begin solving number one?

3. What in the problem and your work led you to believe your chosen answer is correct for number one?

4. Solve: $2x^2 + 9x + 4$.

5. What is the first thing you looked at to begin solving number four?

6. What in the problem and your work led you to believe your chosen answer is correct for number four?

Figure 4.2: Evidence-based mathematics assessment.

To move to an evidence-based grading system, we must create a healthy inventory of evidence-based assessments that capture both outcomes and thinking. Why a student answers correctly is just as important as why he or she didn't choose the other answers.

Evidence-based grading sometimes leads to the mistaken belief that students will be continually tested and assessed because educators need *a lot* of evidence. In reality, it is more important that assessments capture the *right* evidence—instead of a certain *amount* of evidence—at the right time. The right evidence is a natural byproduct of evidence-based assessments. Teachers can ask themselves the following three questions to check if assessments are, in fact, evidence based.

1. **"Do our assessments align with commonly vetted expectations?"** When we base grades on evidence, proficiency-based targets become the assessment's focus. Thus, the assessment itself is nothing more than the byproduct of the *intentional arrangement* of targets in a *singular performance or task event*. O'Connor (2009) states, "If grading plans are approached [like this], the learning goals become the set, and the assessment methods become the subset" (p. 57). This means that teachers must collaboratively vet learning targets before they even begin creating an assessment.

   To vet a target, a team must come to a consensus on how students perceive the proficiency expectation. Learning targets must contain language that describes the performance the team expects and connect to the criteria students must use to be successful. Singletons (teachers without a team) can vet targets with other colleagues in the school or in national or provincial organizations. Likewise, teams should feel compelled to vet targets with students for clarity and understanding.

2. **"Do our assessments contain a commonly vetted structure?"** Next, teams should vet an assessment's structure. As we previously noted, in order for evidence to be the *right* evidence, students must produce it in assessments that teachers create from a gradation of learning (Marzano, 2006).

   Robert J. Marzano (2006) writes that teachers should strive to make assessments one-dimensional and covariant. *One-dimensional* means a *single score* that represents the evidence from a *single target*. *Covariant* means that any targets teachers evaluate during a particular event should supplement each other. In effect, when a student gets better at one target, his or her performance in the other targets potentially improves as well (O'Connor, 2009). Teachers must look at each assessment and decide how it will produce evidence from each gradation of the learning target.

3. **"Do our assessments produce commonly vetted evidence?"** While evidence-based assessments' first two components are commonly overlooked, taking the time to vet the evidence is rarely examined at all. Taking the time to evaluate evidence and calibrate common expectations and methods for interpreting evidence is important to ensuring equity and fairness among teams.

We want to emphasize the importance of creating well-written assessments that demonstrate the relationship between stated curriculum and expectations for learning. A smart assessment structure should reveal curriculum coherence and unity.

Are We Effectively Communicating Learning Targets and Standards?

We should consider the following three questions to ensure that we effectively communicate learning targets.

1. Do students understand the expectations?

2. Do parents understand the expectations?

3. Do colleagues understand the expectations?

Do Students Understand the Expectations?

Rick Stiggins, Judith Arter, Jan Chappuis, and Steve Chappuis (2004) state that "a key feature to student success is students knowing where they are going, that is, understanding what they are to learn" (p. 57). But how do we know whether students truly understand what we expect of them? Aside from directly surveying students, there is no clear way to truly grasp if they understand the learning targets without observing their behavior.

One telling behavior is *language*. If students understand the target, then their language in classroom dialogue—peer to peer and student to teacher—will include the language of the target. Another way to gauge student understanding is *engagement*. Students' physical and cognitive engagement should relate directly to the target's language.

Do Parents Understand the Expectations?

Of all the stakeholders who must understand the expectations, parents and families are the most crucial for overall buy-in. Reporting on targets can help focus parents on the depth and breadth of their children's academic work (Stiggins, 2006).

This can be a delicate process. Parents might not understand the targets' necessity and value if targets are too specific. Broad targets don't tell parents enough about their children's need for growth. Parents of one of our students in a cooking class once told us they didn't care if their child could use a fork correctly; they cared whether their child could practice safe food preparation. In Spanish classes, we often see frustration from parents when the targets are too granular, such as *Conjugate (specific verb)*. Parents say they better understand language that indicates whether their children can *effectively write in Spanish*.

We explain the purpose and criteria of evidence-based grading prior to the beginning of the semester or course to help inform parents. The division director, the team leader, and even the administration acknowledge the policy by endorsing a letter. See a sample letter in figure 4.3.

Explaining the learning targets' purpose and how teachers use them to determine grades is imperative and helps support the implementation of this grading system. We suggest using social media, blogs, and general informational websites to inform the community. We created and use the website Stevenson High School Evidence-Based Reporting (www.myebrexperience.com) to inform our community of policies, practices, and grading system changes.

Do Colleagues Understand the Expectations?

Vetting an expectation with colleagues is one of the most important acts for successfully implementing evidence-based grading. The colleagues we refer to here include fellow teachers, counselors, deans, support staff, student services personnel, tutors, and so on. To keep evidence-based grading less subjective, all educators and supporting faculty members should collaboratively discuss and clearly understand the learning targets, especially when creating and implementing interventions.

Dear Parent or Guardian:

We are excited to inform you that our course will be using evidence-based grading this year. The purpose of evidence-based grading is to ensure that your child's grade truly reflects his or her learning progress. In a traditional grading system, a student's grades on various assignments are averaged. A student who performs poorly early in the semester, but masters all the skills by the end, will still get a lower grade. Evidence-based grading, however, allows us to give grades based on your child's aptitude and growth.

How will we calculate performance with evidence-based grading?

Evidence-based grading focuses on developing proficiencies. These proficiencies are outlined through learning targets. Learning targets are the skills or content that students must master by the end of the course. Throughout the semester, we gather information about your child's skills using the following scale:

4—Exceeds expectations of learning target mastery

3—Demonstrates learning target mastery

2—Is in progress of learning target mastery

1—Is not yet making progress or is making minimal progress toward learning target mastery

Assessments take place at regular intervals during instruction to check for under-standing and mastery of skills.

To let your child grow through the entire semester, the traditional grade calcula-tion of 25 percent for each term and 25 percent for the final exam will **not** be used in this course. Instead, your child will have the opportunity to present evidence of his or her achievement toward each learning target **throughout** the year. Evidence in the second half of the semester will weigh more heavily toward your child's grade. The final exam will still be an important portion of the course.

The final semester grade reflects the proficiency grades for each learning target and standard in the course. Additionally, the teacher will provide feedback for behavior learning standards, although this feedback will not be factored into the final grade.

How do we currently report your child's grade?

You can view an accurate picture of your child's progress toward mastery (using the four-point scale) at any time within the grade portal. Official progress reports and term grades will no longer include letter grades. Instead, they will provide feedback like this:

Adequate growth (AG)—Satisfactory growth with current work

Minimal growth (MG)—Less-than-expected growth; your child will be recom-mended for extra help

Failing (F)—Failure to grow progress

Incomplete (I)—Insufficient evidence

Figure 4.3: Parent letter about an evidence-based grading policy. continued ⟶

We calculate final grades by converting the learning targets to one course grade:

A—A score of 3 or above in **all** standards

B—A score of 2 in any one standard, with a score of 3 or 4 in the remaining standards

C—A score of 2 in more than one standard (no score of 1)

D—A score of 1 in at least one standard, with a score of 2 or above in at least one standard

F—A score of 1 in each standard

Best regards,

Source: Adapted from Lillydahl, 2012.

Effective interventions are based on communicating learning targets to all parties in a school. "Unless a school has clearly identified the essential standards that every student must master . . . it would be nearly impossible to have the curricular focus and targeted assessment data necessary to target interventions" (Buffum, Mattos, & Weber, 2012, p. 137).

We couldn't agree more, and we believe that evidence-based grading allows this to occur. If our own colleagues don't understand what we are asking from students, we allow greater potential for biased assessments and misguided interventions.

Are We Providing Opportunities for Student Growth?

Providing the right opportunities to practice and demonstrate proficiency is one of evidence-based grading's difficult tasks. It might be tempting to simply adopt a task-based assessment framework and overlay a 4, 3, 2, 1 grading scale. However, this does not work. Instead, the change to evidence-based grading requires:

- Creating time to show student growth
- Engaging students in the right practice to promote growth
- Establishing retake opportunities to show growth

Creating Time to Show Student Growth

Traditional sequences provide enough time for students to physically engage with the material but do not necessarily allow the time to process, scrutinize, and reflect on new learning. Students simply need more time than we have traditionally given them to learn from assessments, and this is why retakes are an essential component of evidence-based grading.

By allowing students to continue to learn after exams, we give them time to process their mistakes and rearrange their thinking about a topic to gain new understanding. This is the definition of student growth. If our role as educators is to help students grow, then we must give them time to show us that they are growing. We can do this by placing our summative assessment early in our lesson pacing.

To explain how we can create time for students to grow, we will contrast several learning time lines. Traditional pacing, as shown in figure 4.4, is based on the idea of scaffolding and forces small, segmented portions of learning into discrete components of instruction and assessment. Notice that the summative exam is located at the far end of the time line and does little to help students learn after the evaluation experience (exam). Students learn by reflecting, but after they have already been evaluated.

I = Instruction

Q = Quiz

F = Formative assessment

P = Project

S = Summative exam

R = Retake

Figure 4.4: Traditional learning time line.

This format is not entirely effective for evidence-based courses, as it logistically creates a lot of grading for teachers and forces a pseudo-summative environment—that is, all formative assessments function as mini-summative assessments.

Alternatively, see figure 4.5 for an evidence-based learning time line.

Figure 4.5: Evidence-based learning time line.

Note that the S (summative exam) has moved far up in the pacing and is placed in a position where the stakes are low. There is now more time to retake and learn from mistakes. Without time to reflect after assessments, students find it difficult to achieve growth.

Engaging Students in the Right Practice to Promote Growth

We defined *growth* as learning from mistakes. We do not mean repetitive practice until a student can reach a new level of learning. In their book *Make It Stick*, Brown et al. (2014) discuss the idea of practice. Practice in its most effective form must capture enough of the right evidence, meaningfully connect to a target, and allow for a variety of contexts in which learning can be demonstrated. These three elements allow a student to retrieve the right learning, knowledge, or skill component at the best time to effectively grasp a concept or skill. Brown et al. (2014) discuss three types of practice that are essential to make learning stick.

1. Spaced practice
2. Interwoven practice
3. Varied practice

Let's look at each strategy as it applies to an evidence-based grading system.

Spaced Practice

Massed, condensed practice actually inhibits an evidence-based classroom. In traditional classrooms, fleeting bursts of brilliance are the norm and rely on massed practice (Brown et al., 2014). Massed practice may appear to work, but it doesn't. In *Make It Stick*, Brown et al. (2014) write, "Massed practice gives us the warm sensation of mastery because we're looping information through short-term memory without having to reconstruct the learning from long-term memory" (p. 82).

Spaced practice means that teachers space out mastery performances, including reflective practice or other formative assessment, so students can forget. Brown et al. (2014) state that "the increased effort required to retrieve the learning after a little forgetting has the effect of retriggering consolidation, further strengthening memory" (p. 49). Later, we will explain how to implement this practice.

Teachers in an evidence-based classroom must intentionally pause the learning and inject reflective activities in order for this cycle of forgetting and retrieving to happen.

Interwoven Practice

Interwoven practice means that a teacher teaches multiple targets at the same time. Long-term retention is much better if teachers interweave practice than if they mass it (Brown et al., 2014). Why do teachers hold review sessions? They are reacting to the nature of massed practice. Instead of review sessions, teachers can inject segments that focus on multiple or different targets. Then students can forget, and the demands of retrieving the information increase learning.

Varied Practice

Brown et al. (2014) also discuss their idea of *varied practice*. By this, they don't mean the varied practice we see in modern classrooms, such as reading about a topic, writing about a topic, and then speaking about a topic in one lesson. The variance in evidence-based grading is different. For example, if you have a speech later in the unit, you should speak for the warm-up on day one; the quiz on day three; and the formative assessments on days two, four, and five. While these events are not varied in that they always focus on speaking, they are varied in complexity, structure, context, and so on.

Establishing Retake Opportunities to Show Growth

When dealing with a competency-based platform such as evidence-based grading, retake opportunities are essential. However, teachers tend to apply retakes improperly. Some teachers force retakes into the learning with little regard to time and purpose. Retakes are only useful when students can react to feedback before the retake. Wiliam (2011) states that "feedback functions formatively only if the information fed back to the learner is used by the learner in improving performance" (p. 120). This means that after a performance event, students must have time to digest the feedback for the retake to hold any learning value.

Providing time to react to feedback hinges on quality implementation of retake events. In the following paragraphs, we describe some misconceptions about retakes that we must clarify before proper implementation can occur.

First, teachers sometimes just place a retake on the pacing schedule, essentially communicating that there are two exams for each unit. However, this is wrong. Retakes are a second attempt at learning. This means that the student uses feedback as a prerequisite for the retake. The teacher should not permit the assessment if a student has done nothing to turn feedback from the first exam into knowledge.

Second, a retake is not as simple as taking the test over or giving the full exam again. Instead, students can choose the targets that they need to review and re-perform those to prove they now know them. For example, a social studies paper retake can just ask students to rewrite the last paragraph or pick five lines to change or add.

Last, some teachers still link retakes to behavior—that is, they punish students who do not take the retakes by decreasing the overall grade. Retakes should be the students' choice. Teachers must make students aware of retake opportunities, but they must not chase or force students to take them. And we certainly should not punish students who do not take them by making them worth points. The existence of retakes is essential for evidence-based grading to function properly, but we do not have to force students to complete them.

Are We Separating Academic and Behavior Information in the Gradebook?

Should we report a student's behavior separately from his or her grade? The answer, in short, is *yes*. Guskey and Jung (2013) suggest that we give multiple grades, one for behavior and one for performance growth, and we agree.

What is the difference between the two? *How am I doing?* reflects student achievement. *How am I acting?* reflects student behavior, effort, and work habits. *How am I growing?* reflects what students gain from the learning experience—learning from their mistakes. An evidence-based gradebook should include all three items so it can align with the purpose of letter grades more effectively.

This idea is foreign to some teachers and becomes a struggle for those who have not separated skills from behavior in their idea of school. They may ask, "What about the student who works really hard? Shouldn't he or she get a good grade?" There are many ways that behavior can inadvertently become part of the academic grade, the most common being recording late work, recording missing assignments, and weighting the standards.

Recording Late Work

"Teachers should encourage and support students to submit work on time, but if they do not, teachers should not use penalties" (O'Connor, 2009, pp. 100–101). Instead, in an evidence-based grading system, teachers should record late work as a blank or incomplete as long as there is still time to make up the work.

With that said, late work depends on the concept of target expiration dates. If targets don't expire, or aren't assessed anymore, a realistic and manageable evidence-based environment cannot exist. Many educators wonder if entire semesters should be open for students to submit evidence of their learning at any time. However, this not only is logistically cumbersome but also demotivates students to work at the onset of the course. Teachers should count all work, but only within the expiration window of the target. When the teacher chooses not to evaluate work anymore (the closing of the performance window), then no work is eligible for interpretation.

This is similar to how the Internal Revenue Service (IRS) works. If you do not turn in your tax documents to the IRS by April 15, you will receive a penalty.

Similarly, a teacher should not judge work that students turn in outside the period of time the teacher has dictated. Once that time window closes, he or she stops judging work and, thus, records the assignment as a blank or incomplete in the gradebook.

Inappropriate performance windows can affect student motivation. If the time window is too long, students may not be motivated to learn due to feeling over-confident or bored. The converse is true of too short a window. Students are not motivated because they simply cannot react to the feedback, which may cause them to feel that their performance is out of their hands. In evidence-based grading, communicating performance windows is essential to helping students understand the date by which they must be proficient.

As Thomas R. Guskey and Jane M. Bailey (2001) write, "Rather than attempting to punish students with a low grade or mark in the hope it will prompt greater effort in the future, teachers can better motivate students by considering their work as incomplete and then requiring additional effort" (p. 35). The important connection is that in an evidence-based grading system, if a student does not turn in work and therefore amasses incompletes, he or she must understand that blanks (or patterns of blanks) might mean failure.

Recording Missing Assignments

Some teachers transitioning to evidence-based grading struggle with the idea that they cannot give a zero for assignments that students don't turn in or turn in late. As long as the target expiration window is still open, the mark in the gradebook for missing assignments should remain blank if not assessed yet or be given a code of M (missing and can still be made up). "This sends the message that students must complete the assigned work; they cannot skip assignments and 'take a zero' for them" (Heflebower, Hoegh, & Warrick, 2014, p. 60).

Teachers must hold students who consistently miss expiration windows account-able to complete the work. These students should have a status of *incomplete* until they make up all the work. If the codes of Ms are the most comprehensive evidence in a student's performance portfolio, the student should be at risk of receiving an F at the end of the grading period.

Again, this is similar to how the IRS works. If you do not turn in all your tax documents, the IRS has a hard time determining your taxes. Similarly, a teacher has a hard time determining a grade if he or she does not have all the evidence. An M in the gradebook invites students to make sure that they turn in all evidence.

Parents and guardians are invited to review the Ms in the gradebook to ensure that their student is engaging properly in the curricular experience that is being laid out before them. Engaging parents in the evidence collection always helps ensure that the student's portfolio is complete and ready for review by the teacher.

Weighting the Standards

Remember, standards are the grade givers—they state the skills students must master. Learning targets help students break down those expectations and work toward meeting the standards. Learning targets allow us to collect evidence, and the standards package that information for effective communication of learning.

In an evidence-based grading system, we don't consider certain tasks more important than others. But we can look at the standards to decide which group of *targets* is more important than others. O'Connor (2009) emphasizes this point when he says, "It is very important that weighting reflect the intent and emphasis on different learning goals/assessments in the final grade" (p. 159).

For example, suppose a teacher states that in order to get an A, students must have a 4 in a particular standard. Teachers must decide which standard students should focus on based on the course, department, or district's mission or purpose, but only if necessary. O'Connor (2009) goes on to say, "The rule of thumb should be that unless differential weighting obviously is needed, all categories are of equal weight" (p. 159).

The way we see it, all work is of equal weight as it relates to the learning target. This means that the warm-up, the quiz, and the test sections that relate to the learning target all provide evidence of student learning and understanding and, therefore, should receive the same weight. Riding a bike down your driveway or down the street or around the block is all still riding a bike.

Are We Ensuring Student Accountability?

Some leaders and stakeholders might ask, "Is evidence-based grading good for students?" This question is difficult to answer, as there are many different viewpoints on what variables make evidence-based grading successful. More important, we can only consider it successful if we hold students responsible for demonstrating their learning. This is where the evidence is produced.

As O'Connor (2007b) puts it, "We are faced with the irony that a policy [traditional grading] that may be grounded in the belief of holding students accountable (giving zeros) actually allows some students to escape accountability for learning" (p. 96). Evidence-based grading attempts to create responsibility and self-reliance in our students through three avenues.

1. Homework

2. Grades

3. Content

Responsibility for Homework

Homework is a major concern of evidence-based grading models. Historically, teachers have used homework as a form of compliance—they give a grade just for completing it. Many experts believe that the simple act of doing homework does not necessarily translate into increased performance or learning (Kohn, 2006; Vatterott, 2009).

In evidence-based grading, we can view homework in two ways: as a piece of evidence eligible for interpretation or as formative practice. If the teacher chooses to mobilize homework as the former, then he or she should tell students that their homework is eligible for judgment and goes into the gradebook.

However, if the teacher mobilizes homework as formative practice, then he or she should carefully and intentionally determine when it is necessary for learning. As one of our teachers, Mike Martinez, says, "In evidence-based grading, I don't give homework a lot, but when I do, it is very intentionally connected to what proficiency we are trying to develop" (personal communication, March 15, 2015). Either way works, but teachers must be deliberate about which method they use for homework and communicate that to their students.

In order for homework to function properly in an evidence-based system, students must see it as a self-evaluation tool, an effective mechanism to determine where they are in relation to the learning targets. In other words, homework must act as formative assessment (Vatterott, 2015).

Responsibility for Grades

"The standards-based grading paradigm changes the game in several ways. First, only learning is graded" (Vatterott, 2015, p. 36). Grades represent one thing—a student's mastery of academic expectations. No one focuses on points or rewards. A student must work to achieve mastery, and the grade represents the level to which the student has done so.

However, while we might not be able to fully banish students' obsession with letter grades, we might be able to significantly lessen it. At the high school level, we see letter grades as permanent. Students need to know their grades for college admission and other societal expectations. We're OK with this—it's a fact of life. So it is extremely important that we inform students about their grades without taking away from the focus on proficiency-based targets or standards.

Ideally, students would use proficiency-based targets to determine their progress, but we can combine both scenarios. See the digital gradebook in figure 4.6 (page 118), which shows a grading trajectory. Teachers should base grades in an evidence-based course on a grading trajectory, not a single grade. Therefore, we

Course	Grade Trajectory	Standard	Bimodal Scores	Proficiency Score	Raw Counts 4, 3, 2, 1
6-SPA301	A/B	Interpersonal communication	3/2	3	2/10/5/2
		Interpretive skills	3/4	4	7/6/2/3
		Presentational communication	3/4	4	10/11/5/7
		Responsible decision making	3/2	3	5/12/14/3
		Self-awareness and self-management	3/2	3	6/15/13/2

Figure 4.6: Evidence-based grading trajectory.

place students on A/B, B/C, C/D, or F trajectories. This reduces the focus on grades just enough to allow teacher-student conversations to be a bigger part of the learning process.

Responsibility for Content

Some teachers share a general uneasiness that course content has disappeared in an evidence-based grading system, or that evidence-based grading is only based on skills. While teachers write the learning targets with actions in mind, content knowledge is still essential. Teachers simply repurpose it into a supporting role to a target. Content knowledge cannot be the expectation itself. Students must *do* something to show that they know the content. Brown et al. (2014) highlight this point when they write, "Conceptual knowledge requires an understanding of the interrelationships of the basic elements [what teachers know as content] within a larger structure that enable them to function together" (p. 55). When a student demonstrates learning through doing, the student evidences skills that exceed mere mimicry.

You may be asking how this can be. Teachers are used to thinking that students just need to know content. If we look more closely at an assessment that verifies student content knowledge (for example, a multiple-choice exam), we might see that instead of demonstrating that students *know* content, it demonstrates that students are able to *recognize* content when given choices.

Let's look at an example in which students must write an answer to a question from a scenario. This still does not demonstrate students' ability to *know* content; it demonstrates that students can provide details and context through writing *using* content. Content in both scenarios takes a *supporting role* to the target—recognizing and providing details. Brown et al. (2014) conclude that using content in a supporting role allows students to "go beyond the acquisition of simple forms of knowledge and reach into the higher sphere of comprehension" (p. 55). Having students make a connection between what is expected of them (learning target) and the supporting criteria and content connected to the expectation is a critical component of evidence-based learning.

Are We Creating Effective Evidence-Based Gradebooks?

Setting up the gradebook for evidence-based grading can be challenging. We offer several options for setting up evidence-based gradebooks, including focuses on events, growth, and proficiency.

Figure 4.7 shows an event-focused gradebook that does not center on the time period of developing proficiency but rather on discrete tasks. This is the closest relative to traditional gradebooks, since it focuses on the tasks teachers ask students to perform to achieve a certain learning target. This structure displays growth determined by a collection of events as opposed to overall growth during a time period of learning. We recommend this heavily task-based gradebook format for mathematics, science, English, and applied arts courses.

Standard 1											
Student Name	Target 1			Target 2				Target 3				Growth Score
	Event 1	Event 2	Event 3	Event 1	Event 2	Event 3	Event 4	Event 1	Event 2	Event 3	Event 4	Score
Dan	2	2	3	3	3	4	3	3	3	4	3	AG
Ming	3	3	3	3	3	3	2	3	3	3	3	MG
Ronnie	2	1	3	3	2	2	2	1	2	2	2	AG
Dana	3	2	3	3	2	2	2	3	3	2	3	F

Figure 4.7: Event-focused gradebook.

continued ⟶

Social-Emotional Learning			
Student Name	Week 1	Week 2	Week 3
Dan	3	3	3
Ming	3	2	3
Ronnie	3	4	4
Dana	3	2	1

Figure 4.8 shows the second gradebook option and is based on the principle of growth. Everything is organized by time period for proficiency development. Students develop proficiency during that time, and once it has passed, their proficiency is locked in. This banking is due to changing content themes or contexts that don't necessarily relate to each other. While the expected proficiency may be the same during each time period, the context in which it develops might change. For example, suppose an English class moves from reading books about fictional themes to nonfiction texts. The target of citing evidence in a text accurately is still the proficiency expectation; however, students now develop it within a new context. We recommend this gradebook format for world language, English, and social studies courses.

Standard 1												
Student Name	Event 1			Event 2				Event 3				Growth Score
	Target 1	Target 2	Target 3	Target 1	Target 2	Target 3	Target 4	Target 1	Target 2	Target 3	Target 4	Score
Dan	2	2	3	3	3	4	3	3	3	4	3	AG
Ming	3	3	3	3	3	3	2	3	3	3	3	MG
Ronnie	2	1	3	3	2	2	2	1	2	2	2	AG
Dana	3	2	3	3	2	2	2	3	3	2	3	F

Social-Emotional Learning			
Student Name	Week 1	Week 2	Week 3
Dan	3	3	3
Ming	3	2	3
Ronnie	3	4	4
Dana	3	2	1

Figure 4.8: Growth-focused gradebook.

Finally, figure 4.9 (page 122) shows a proficiency-focused gradebook that uses the evidence-based principle of taking the most recent score. This gradebook gives no consideration to where a student starts; it focuses on where a student ends up. The number that represents *current* proficiency is the only concern. We recommend this gradebook format for performance-based courses such as fine arts, physical education, and applied arts.

In order for the gradebook to function as an effective feedback tool for students, families, and other stakeholders, students must be able to answer these three questions.

1. How am I growing? (growth)

2. How am I doing? (proficiency)

3. How am I behaving? (social-emotional learning)

If evidence-based grading is based on these three components, then gradebooks should reflect these same three components. Figure 4.10 (pages 122–123) is an evidence-based gradebook that includes growth, proficiency, and social-emotional learning.

How Am I Growing?

The gradebook must contain an area to track student growth. This simply means reporting on how the student is keeping up with the academic challenges of the course. This area is based on observation, interaction, and evidence of performance. Figure 4.10 shows where teachers can report on this area.

Standard 1											
Student Name	Objective 1			Objective 2				Objective 3				Growth Score
	Target 1	Target 2	Target 3	Target 1	Target 2	Target 3	Target 4	Target 1	Target 2	Target 3	Target 4	Score
Dan	2	2	3	3	3	4	3	3	3	4	3	AG
Ming	3	3	3	3	3	3	2	3	3	3	3	MG
Ronnie	2	1	3	3	2	2	2	1	2	2	2	AG
Dana	3	2	3	3	2	2	2	3	3	2	3	F

Social-Emotional Learning			
Student Name	Week 1	Week 2	Week 3
Dan	3	3	3
Ming	3	2	3
Ronnie	3	4	4
Dana	3	2	1

Figure 4.9: Proficiency-focused gradebook.

Standard 1											
Student Name	Learning Target 1			Learning Target 2				Learning Target 3				Growth Score
	Event 1	Event 2	Event 3	Event 1	Event 2	Event 3	Event 4	Event 1	Event 2	Event 3	Event 4	Score
Dan	2	2	3	3	3	4	3	3	3	4	3	AG

Ming	3	3	3	3	3	3	2	3	3	3	3	MG
Ronnie	2	1	3	3	2	2	2	1	2	2	2	AG
Dana	3	2	3	3	2	2	2	3	3	2	3	F

Social-Emotional Learning			
Student Name	Week 1	Week 2	Week 3
Dan	3	3	3
Ming	3	2	3
Ronnie	3	4	4
Dana	3	2	1

Figure 4.10: Evidence-based gradebook.

How Am I Doing?

This question reports on aptitude. An effective, evidence-based gradebook needs to answer the question, How is the student doing with course material and skill development? In this area, teachers report on each student's aptitude with a 1–4 scale based on the learning target's gradation. This area outlines each learning target and each event teachers use to gather evidence on each target.

How Am I Behaving?

The last area focuses on how students are acting and behaving in the course. While the debate continues about whether it is the school's responsibility to assess behavior or leave it as corollary to academic learning, we can all agree that we should report it separately. Figure 4.10 shows how the gradebook appears with social-emotional learning targets as the basis for gathering evidence.

O'Connor (2009) summarizes evidence-based grading's value as follows:

> Teachers should stop using points and percentages and use clearly described, criterion-referenced (or absolute) performance standards based on proficiency with a limited number of levels that are public, based on expert knowledge, clearly stated in words or numbers, and supported by exemplars or models. (p. 86)

Teachers can achieve this by grading based on learning targets and proficiencies instead of points; by giving feedback instead of grades; and by providing students, families, colleagues, and others narrative information about a student's learning.

Key Points

Evaluating an evidence-based grading model's effectiveness considers the interrelationship among well-written curriculum, expectations, and the assessments that collect evidence and allow students to demonstrate skills. Evaluating that interrelationship is a compelling way to collaborate with teammates, as it challenges us to generate a viable and guaranteed curriculum. The process demonstrates equities and inequities, and it holds us accountable to every student's success. Review the following key points from this chapter to ensure you firmly grasp the content.

- Evidence-based grading requires the opportunity for students to retake exams if they so choose.

- Evidence-based grading requires that instruction interweaves and varies practice associated with learning targets.

- Evidence-based grading assessments must capture both outcomes and thinking.

- Teachers should format the gradebook to capture and communicate proficiency rather than tasks.

Chapter 5

Elaboration

A commitment to continuous improvement is one of the most valuable mindsets in education. School cultures must embrace this belief system as a commitment toward change. As educators, we must model what it means to change, to grow, to learn, and to improve. That's what school is all about.

As our team moves forward in its work, continuous improvement is the topic of its conversations around the value of evidence-based grading, teaching, and learning. Within this phase, the team considers smarter revisions to its approach to evidence-based grading, and it develops other ideas around how an evidence-based model can make an impact on more unified relationships among curriculum, instruction, and assessment.

The elaboration phase—like all the other phases in the creative process—does not operate independently from the preparation, incubation, insight, and evaluation phases. It operates in conjunction with these phases. During the creative process, elaboration means to build up an idea, tweak it, give it nuance, and develop the idea's full potential.

In this phase, our team questions, brainstorms, and gains new insights it thinks might help improve its work with curriculum, instruction, and assessment. While the team continues to elaborate on the work it's doing, pay attention to how team members position and reposition their thinking and ideas for better implementation.

Following are three key points to remember during the elaboration phase.

1. The elaboration phase is about continuously improving how evidence-based grading can align curriculum, instruction, and assessment.

Elaboration can be about fine-tuning learning targets or bringing more nuance to how expectations are stated to challenge student learning.

2. During this phase, team members recognize the value of evidence-based grading, but they want to build on its success and make needed revisions to ensure *all* students can succeed. At this point, team members are ready to serve as teacher leaders, sharing their struggles and successes with other teacher teams.

3. As the process of evidence-based grading leads to continuous improvement, all students should benefit from the team's collective and collaborative wisdom. Schools should value the collaborative process as a means to continually evaluate and improve on new ideas for achievement.

Our Team's Story

Mario feels great because of the work his team has accomplished in a year's time. Moving to evidence-based grading is no small feat, and he looks back on the year and the huge impact the change made on teaching and learning. The team has one more meeting, and Mario reviews the results from a recent student survey about implementing evidence-based grading to prepare.

Mario organizes the data and creates a protocol to review them with his team. As team members enter the room, they seem somber. Mario, gauging his team's mood, decides to start the meeting with a simple question. "Everything OK?"

Britney speaks first. "I'm not sure it's working . . . evidence-based grading, I mean."

"Why's that?" Mario asks. He is confused because the data are very positive.

"I don't know," Britney replies. "I just feel like my students aren't learning. I mean, my final exam scores were low the first semester, and I feel like we aren't getting through all the material."

Mario is about to answer, but Kevin says, "I'm having the same trouble. I took a poll in my classes last month, and my students all said they struggled with the evidence-based grading system. It's hard enough to teach them the curriculum content. Why are we trying to teach them in a way that seems difficult to them?"

Maya adds, "I'm getting the same feedback. I thought I was alone in thinking that."

Mario seizes this opportunity to start the data discussion. "What if I told you that from the thousands of students we surveyed throughout our school, three times as many students like it as dislike it?"

Silence fills the room. Seeing no one is going to answer, Mario says, "And in social studies, five times as many students like it as dislike it. This means that out of a class of thirty, twenty-five students like it."

Joni says, "I think my students are starting to like it, but not all of them."

Mario brings another piece of data to the table. "It is interesting to note that we all gave the same number of A grades, meaning each of us gave 40 percent As in our classes."

"Really? That surprises me," Kevin says.

Britney says, "But it is easier to get an A now than in a traditional grading course. We are giving too many As."

Mario says, "Britney, that actually isn't true. Looking at the entire student body, students in evidence-based courses receive the same distribution of grades. While we do give slightly more As, we are only within a few percent of non-evidence-based courses each semester."

These data surprise the group. Mario passes out the survey and achievement data. "I want to review these data because we should but also to celebrate our work all year. This is really hard work. It can be confusing and even tense at times, but we did it. We were successful! Yes, we still have work to do, but we were successful. Our students are learning . . . and learning better."

The team first reviews data showing that student achievement is up a few percentage points in an aggregate of all class scores, and the percentage of students mastering targets is up a few percentage points as well.

Kevin says, "But we don't know. This could have just been because the group was smarter this year."

Mario has done his homework. "I checked this year's entrance exam scores and compared them to last year's, and they score the same," he says. "Also, I have information that clarifies that fewer students dropped the course this year than in years past. Moreover, students from our course who received an intervention did not get lower than a C in the course."

"That's great!" Maya exclaims.

Mario continues, "Also, like I said earlier, according to the survey, five times as many students like the evidence-based grading system as dislike it. I think sometimes we draw conclusions from a few students who don't represent the whole group.

"But I would still like to review certain aspects of the survey. Even with the high rate of positive responses, 15 percent of our students do not like the new system. So, I would like to explore their narrative responses on the survey."

Mario produces a summary sheet that contains the most frequent responses from the survey for each level of the Likert scale. Level 1 is for students who dislike the change, and level 5 is for students who like the change. Following are the survey data.

- **Level 1:** Seven percent of students said, "I don't understand it at all (rules and grade calculation)."

- **Level 2:** Thirteen percent of students said, "It's hard to get an A now."

- **Level 3:** Twenty-six percent of students said, "I like the system, but it takes too much time to figure out how I'm doing."

- **Level 4:** Thirty-three percent of students said, "It makes sense and is fair."

- **Level 5:** Twenty-one percent of students said, "It is fairer than traditional grading, and I can recover from failures."

After giving the team a few minutes to review the data, Mario asks, "Why is it that 7 percent of our students stated they don't understand it?"

Britney answers, "I think it is because they can't figure out that grading is based on modes of evidence."

"Why is it so hard to figure out modes?" Maya questions.

"Because they are used to accumulating points and getting as many as possible," Kevin replies.

Joni asks, "Why are they still thinking this way?"

Mario says, "I think it might be because our assessment structure still promotes that a 4 is an A."

"Why do you think our assessment structure promotes a scaled 4 as an A grade?" Britney asks.

"Because we give a 4 if they get a certain number of questions correct. Why do we do that?" Kevin says.

"Because our assessments are not balanced. We don't have parts that capture evidence of all levels," Joni replies.

Kevin says, "Yeah, our assessments are basically only three-level questions, and we simply grade based on how many three-level questions a student gets correct. That doesn't give us evidence except for level 3. We need to add level-2 and level-4 questions as well."

Mario jots down some notes. When he looks up, he finds the group smiling—smiling because it has come full circle. Team members have implemented a new grading system and are now working logically and collaboratively to make it even better.

This culture of elaboration will remain with the team for years, and regardless of who enters or leaves the team, elaborating on evidence-based grading will be the norm.

The Six Core Beliefs in Evidence-Based Grading

Even at the elaboration phase of development, it takes an incredible amount of energy and focus to maintain this level of practice. An elaborative practice moves at the same rate as experimental action and insightful reflection, but it is also a different experience altogether. At this point, team members add nuance to and extend ideas and evolve in their thinking.

Teachers must approach the elaboration phase boldly, committing to the idea that every assertion is potentially a new insight in disguise. This phase is filled with many new opinions to manage and thresholds to cross. That is why the key to this phase is to manage all the considerations that now exist due to the other phases' work. During elaboration, a team should hold the work to fidelity but improve on that sturdy foundation.

In our story, the team members begin to make new assertions about teaching and learning through their experience with evidence-based grading and to focus on the six core beliefs of this practice.

1. Evidence is more precise than any formula.

2. We determine what students deserve.

3. We never fully realize curriculum without evidence-based practice.

4. Evidence-based grading improves team collaboration.

5. Communication with the community is essential.

6. We must take a postsecondary perspective.

Evidence Is More Precise Than Any Formula

An algorithm is never as precise as an expert interpreting the evidence. While formulas might make a teacher's job of assessing students easier, they don't make it more accurate. We argue that it is *less* accurate. As Guskey (2015) emphasizes, the "mathematical algorithms teachers use in determining students' grades provide only the illusion of precision and objectivity" (p. 95).

An algorithm, no matter how precise it appears, has a higher chance of unfairly categorizing a student than if the teacher and student co-construct the evidence and deliberate on it together (Guskey, 2015). Learning co-construction is one foundational principle of evidence-based grading. In successful evidence-based grading, classroom teachers rely on evidence as their script for feedback, leverage for motivating students, resource for creating quality instruction, template for assessment, and basis for accurate and meaningful grade calculation.

However simple it may sound to interpret the evidence from exams to determine a grade, it is still difficult to implement because many elements of student performance appear to require subjective interpretation. This is actually not true. There are several subtle yet undeniable elements of student performance that can help a teacher transition to evidence-based grading successfully. These elements include the following.

- Student performance has a central tendency or pattern.
- Student performance has a trajectory.
- Student performance has context.

Student Performance Has a Central Tendency or Pattern

In evidence-based grading, student performance has a central tendency, and we should view any outliers as irrelevant. Just like in traditional grading, outliers can have a huge impact on the grade if teachers average them in, distorting the final grade (O'Connor, 2011). In our experience, teachers often ignore the preponderance of evidence, or the central tendency, because they believe averaging more precisely evaluates student performance. We disagree.

Many alternatives exist to determine the central tendency of student performance, but teachers rarely use them because of the myth that mathematics offers more precise clarity around student learning. We must free ourselves from this myth and have confidence in our professionalism and knowledge in grading. Guskey (2015) suggests three possibilities to determine central tendency: (1) the most recent evidence, (2) the most comprehensive evidence, and (3) the most important evidence, or all three.

While we agree that these are effective grading practices, even these can feel subjective to many. Of these three, the one that works best for us is using the most comprehensive evidence. However, let's go a step further and consider what *supports* the most comprehensive evidence to provide a clear picture of student learning. That is, what is the second most comprehensive pattern of evidence? Without extending our scope in this way, we risk improperly classifying students.

Consider the following two students. The first student scores 92, 93, 80, 93, 90, 92, 80, 90, 92, and 91. Based on the most comprehensive evidence, the first student clearly gets an A. The second student scores 95, 64, 65, 94, 90, 92, 65, 60, 93, and 91. What grade would you give the second student? There are six instances of an A, yet there are four instances of a D+ or lower. This is why teachers tend to rely on an average—cases like these are challenging. If we just look at the most comprehensive scores, the grade is an A, but it is also supported by D work. So, does an A seem like an accurate grade?

If we convert these two scenarios to evidence-based scores, it is much easier to determine an accurate grade. The first student scores 3, 2, 3, 2, 3, 3, 3, 3, 2, 2, and 3. The first student would get a 3 based on the preponderance of scores. Here, the student evidenced a preponderance of 3s. He has proficient scores as well as approaching-proficient scores. This leads to a preponderance of proficiency supported by approaching proficiency. So, this student could have an A or a B.

The second student scores 3, 3, 1, 1, 3, 3, 3, 3, 1, 1, and 3. The second student would also get a 3 based on the fact that 3 is the most common score. But is that the right score for this student? Many non-proficient scores support the proficient scores. This leads to a preponderance of proficiency that non-proficiency supports. So, would this student still earn an A or a B?

In these evidence-based scenarios, teachers do not average the evidence; they must *interpret* it. This means that a teacher might deem the proficiency that the second student demonstrates as shaky and, therefore, assign him or her a different final grade than the first student, maybe a B or a C.

In order to reduce the time it takes to review all the student evidence in a teacher's caseload, we developed a bimodal proficiency matrix (see figure 5.1) to help sort through all the eligible student evidence that appears in an evidence-based gradebook. This matrix allows teachers to quickly interpret the most comprehensive evidence, along with supporting evidence, and assign a proficiency ranking to each student under the respective standard. (Visit **go.SolutionTree.com /assessment** to download a free reproducible version of this figure.)

4	3	2	1
4–3	2–4	2–3	1–4
4–2	3–2	2–1	1–3
3–4	4–1	3–1	1–2

Figure 5.1: Bimodal proficiency matrix.

While this matrix works for our needs, we recognize that it may not work for everyone. So we invite readers to make their own bimodal matrix if this matrix doesn't fit their needs. Figure 5.2 (page 132) shows an alternative matrix in which the 2–4 and 3–1 combinations are switched. (Visit **go.SolutionTree.com /assessment** to download a free reproducible version of this figure.)

4	3	2	1
4–3	3–1	2–3	1–4
4–2	3–2	2–1	1–3
3–4	4–1	2–4	1–2

Figure 5.2: Alternative bimodal proficiency matrix.

This matrix offers educators a quick and effective way to consider not only the most comprehensive evidence but also supporting evidence. Please keep in mind that this is not a mathematical formula and must not be treated as such. It is simply a tool for teachers to project what the evidence suggests. Ultimately, the teacher's interpretation of all the evidence dictates the student's grade (Guskey, 2015). We acknowledge that interpreting central tendency is difficult and time-consuming. However, using the most comprehensive evidence along with evidence that supports it is the most accurate way to classify student performance.

Student Performance Has a Trajectory

Even after a teacher finds the pattern of performance, or the central tendency, he or she must further review the evidence to determine the student growth trajectory. Is the student keeping pace with all the course's academic challenges? Is the student failing to grow? Stagnating? Or is the student reversing growth over time? Guskey and Jung (2013) call this idea *progress criteria*.

Growth is an essential and determining factor in students' grades within an evidence-based system. If the student demonstrates a recent and obvious trajectory or pattern, then the teacher should consider the more recent scores. If there is no clear growth trajectory, then the preponderance of scores and evidence determines the proficiency and grade. A volatile trajectory with varied scores and no evident pattern means growth scores might look like the following: A student scores 3, 2, 3, 3, 2, 2, 3, 3, 2, 3, 2, and 3. This student has no clear pattern of growth or decline, and thus, the matrix score of 3–2 would apply, resulting in a 3 (proficient) score for this student.

If the trajectory is flat, meaning the student maintains a given level of proficiency throughout the course, then the growth score will be 0. We can interpret this to mean that the student maintains this level of proficiency and must be rewarded with that proficiency score. This scenario will look something like the following: A student scores 3, 3, 3, 3, 2, 3, 3, 3, 2, 3, 2, and 3. It's important to understand that each student's learning has its own unique trajectory and must be considered when determining a grade.

Student Performance Has Context

It should be obvious to educators that students don't learn and perform in a vacuum. No matter how much external evaluation systems, software development companies, and state mandates may make it feel like they do, it is simply false. The belief that we can capture student learning through software or proprietary formulas undermines the whole idea of learning. They cannot capture many factors, both internal and external, that contribute to learning. Watching a student perform and grow has a personal and environmental context.

Suppose a student takes a test that the teacher makes a bit too challenging. When reviewing the assessment, the teacher decides to drop a question because he or she realizes it was too confusing or the material that it pertains to was not properly covered in class.

Now that the teacher drops the question and adjusts the scores, what does an A on that test represent? How can one confidently look at the A and interpret that mark's significance? On the other hand, students are allowed retakes in an evidence-based grading system. This retake means that context can be less of a variable in the learning formula.

We Determine What Students Deserve

After hearing that she was supposed to determine a student's grade by interpreting the evidence, a teacher once told us, "Who am I to say what the student gets?" We are shocked as we continue to speak with teachers across the United States at how many still share this sentiment, that a gradebook, an external entity, can better assess their students and even give the students a grade better than the teacher can.

With that said, many teachers we work with seem to be hesitant about evidence-based grading, as the task of interpreting evidence can be daunting. They might ask, "How, with a course load of one hundred students, will I be able to interpret all student evidence?" There are many nuances in grading that may lead teachers to feel insecure or doubtful when determining student grades. Knowing more about these nuances bolsters teachers' confidence in using evidence to determine grades. We highlight a few here.

Blips in Performance

When looking at students with a proficiency-based focus, we are more likely to see blips in performance than with averaging. This is due to students rising to or retreating from different levels of understanding. For example, a student can write effective arguments to support claims in text analysis, using valid reasoning and relevant and sufficient evidence. But in a later unit, he or she can only cite textual evidence using valid reasoning, but the evidence is not relevant. Accounting for these blips is important to maintaining a clear grading policy in an evidence-based classroom.

Teachers often do not think about these blips because traditional grading practices hide them behind the aggregation of earned points for each assessment. Students don't see emergent skills separately from the assessment, nor do teachers view student learning that way. Furthermore, an averaging-based system promotes these flashes of brilliance and can even accept them as complete knowledge or skill attainment (Schoemaker, 2011).

In contrast, in an evidence-based grading system, teachers have the ability to note these blips early and deal with them promptly. When blips occur, the matrix waits until a result (or score) becomes a preponderance before considering it as part of a student's proficiency. However, depending on when the blip occurs, the teacher may decide it has sufficient context and, thus, this score represents the student's proficiency. The preponderance is always first in our view. Ultimately, evidence-based grading asks teachers to judge students on patterns of growth, not brief moments of brilliance.

Absenteeism

In traditional classrooms, a common yet unwritten norm among teachers states that students who do not attend class for any given reason can receive a zero to motivate them to show up. This is still a common practice, despite research on zero scores' detrimental effect on learning (Guskey, 2013).

Luckily, zeros don't mean anything in an evidence-based grading system. If a student is absent, the teacher records an *incomplete* to show that the student has not shown mastery—yet.

Incompletes

A common anxiety producer for teachers is what to do with students who simply don't do the work. The "punishment" for not doing work in evidence-based classrooms is doing the work. However, this is difficult to manage in reality, as many of our teachers have stated. Some students simply don't care, and chasing them around is time-consuming. The reality is that some students just don't do the work and need consequences, such as failing the course. Again, if *incomplete* is one of the two modal matrix scores, then the teacher must give a grade of F. A student with a pattern of blanks risks failing.

All Evidence

In our experience, just using the most recent evidence never accurately portrays the student's achievement and learning. Teachers must take into account the most recent scores but not assume they represent a growth pattern. A very clear pattern of growth or decline means the most recent score has a higher probability of being correct. Many teachers review all evidence if the most recent scores differ from the pattern that immediately preceded them. We find that a focus on most recent scores can cause a lack of student motivation early in the semester. The fact that the grade is solely based on growth demotivates early learning. But teachers who use growth in conjunction with recent evidence achieve the best balance to determine a grade.

Final Exams

Final exams are a tricky topic in evidence-based grading. Most teachers view the final exam as a living, breathing determinant of a student's learning. Some teachers look to final exams to tell them what grade a student should get. Some teachers hold the final exam in such high regard that it's like an oracle that determines a student's past, present, and future.

In evidence-based grading, the final exam has no more weight than anything else because it aligns to a learning target. Wait . . . *what?*

The final exam has the same importance and weight as a warm-up on day three? Yes. In evidence-based grading, we don't discriminate based on task. Proficiency is proficiency whether it is an exit slip, a quiz, an exam, or even the final exam. Since the final exam aligns to targets in the same way as a warm-up or homework assignment, we can view it as essentially the last piece of evidence for a given set of targets.

We illustrate this point with an example. A team of mathematics teachers decided to upend its final exam process. It uses the final exam in a formative way by moving up the assessment in its pacing and employing the traditional final exam time for evidence review or retake activities. Students get an average grade for each term, and the teacher averages those grades with the final exam grade.

In evidence-based grading, the teacher reviews the semester evidence first and then runs through the matrix for each learning target of the course. If a student fails to reach proficiency in even one target, he or she is eligible to take the formative exams. These exams are essentially a retake of the standards the student did not master.

After this event, if a student still hasn't mastered a standard, he or she is eligible to take the non-mastered standards on final exam day. Students who have mastered the standards and do not need the final exam retake must review their portfolios of work with the teacher and confirm the final semester grade. This approach has built-in opportunities for growth and recovery. It also minimizes the high-stakes effect that a final exam has on learning.

We Never Fully Realize Curriculum Without Evidence-Based Practice

Teachers and teams have labored over curriculum for hundreds of years and still continue to refine it. These improvements come at a cost—time, effort, confusion, improper implementation, and so on. When teachers implement evidence-based grading, it exposes real curriculum issues. What we mean is that until teachers must rely on common assessments and learning standards to give a student a grade, they will never fully realize the strengths or weaknesses of their curriculum. By implementing evidence-based grading, a teacher can gain full control of his or her curriculum: awareness of expectations, intentionality, and the role of content.

Awareness of Expectations

We must resist the urge to wait for some external body, such as a national or provincial organization, to guide us to our expected curriculum. Instead, clarify expectations, vet them with colleagues, and align them with the national or provincial organization. In evidence-based grading, we must start with our inherent knowledge and specified training in the content areas to build a healthy, guaranteed, and viable curriculum based on proficiency-based learning targets. The following are four questions to guide this work.

1. **What is the teachers' definition of quality for this topic?** When asked how a student can show proficiency, teachers will likely respond with a variety of terms, adjectives, and ideas to use to create proficiency-based learning targets. For example, a teacher might use terms like *creative* or *detailed*.

2. **What does the end product look like?** With teachers focused on so many other tasks, such as curriculum mapping, lesson planning, and best practices, it is sometimes difficult for them to articulate what they *ideally* want from students. By asking teachers to describe what the end product looks like, the language that they produce often represents a proficiency-based learning target.

3. **What is the purpose of this work?** This is an essential discussion point when developing learning targets. When teachers articulate their intent for the work, they can help clarify what is expected, making teaching and learning more explicit to students.

4. **How will teachers measure this work?** Asking teachers to describe the assessment can draw out the hidden language of proficiency, and it allows them to hear the proficiency-based target beginning to form. Teachers generally embed their expectations in their assessments, so we must draw out those expectations. This question helps teachers see the path to proficiency, and the description of this pathway helps lead to the development of learning targets (Gobble et al., 2016).

Intentionality

In evidence-based grading, teachers must be intentional at all times. This means finding ways to deliberately control the lesson to provide periods of intense cognitive engagement followed by periods that allow students to forget the material, thus increasing retrieval potency when they return to cognitive engagement (Brown et al., 2014).

This idea of *allowing for forgetting* means that upon returning to direct learning of specific content or skills, students strengthen new ideas and give them meaning while connecting them to other learning. This process is known as *consolidation* (Brown et al., 2014). When a teacher intentionally pauses a lesson by interweaving other practices, perhaps other learning standards or targets, he or she promotes consolidation upon returning to the initial content. This leads to stronger mental models and learning, which furthers retention of information and skills (Brown et al., 2014).

Along with lesson pausing to reflect on what occurred, teachers can intentionally delay aspects of the lesson to permit more rigor in students' material retrieval (Brown et al., 2014). Teachers in evidence-based classrooms achieve this delay by interweaving other practices that capture different types of evidence on other targets but don't necessarily relate to the main objective for the day. This means teachers must plan lessons that include learning targets that possess a covariance (Marzano, 2006) and interweave them to balance practice and intentional pausing. Covariance means that if a student gets better at one particular skill and other skills increase in proficiency as well, then those skills are covariant. In our experience, covariant targets and skills increase consolidation and long-lasting learning.

Some ideas for interweaving instruction include (Brown et al., 2014):

- Low-stakes formative quizzing and self-assessing

- Embedded reflective pauses

- Varied practice of related targets

- Problem solving before teaching the solution

The Role of Content

The following information is from our personal experience of quality instruction and assessment. We believe that this information is critical to having a fully functioning evidence-based system. Full control over content means that lessons shift away from a traditional grading system to an evidence-based grading system that requires students to consolidate supporting skills or content into stronger, more contextualized learning. In a mimicry-based model, teachers expect students to master supporting content *before* proceeding to the proficiency demonstration. In evidence-based classrooms, teachers give students full control of the supporting content early on and immediately ask them to perform tasks related to the targeted proficiency. For example, suppose we are in a construction class. Figure 5.3 shows the learning targets for the course in a traditional learning pathway.

Learning Target 1	Learning Target 2	Learning Target 3	Learning Target 4	Learning Target 5
I can use a hammer.	I can use a nail.	I can use a screwdriver.	I can use a screw.	I can hang drywall.

Figure 5.3: Learning targets in a traditional learning pathway.

A teacher using this model does not give control of these elements to students and simply ask them to master each target separately before moving on to the next. In an evidence-based classroom, however, the teacher would plan a lesson that interweaves these elements together with practice and reflection, knowing full well that as a student's ability to hang drywall increases, so do his or her knowledge and skills of using a hammer, nail, screw, and screwdriver.

Furthermore, the teacher in the evidence-based classroom would not need to verify that each student knows how to use a hammer or nail before assessing the seemingly bigger skill of hanging drywall. The task of hanging drywall would lead students to consolidate their learning of the hammer, nail, screw, and screwdriver faster and more purposefully than if they simply began this practice with learning about the hammer, then the nail, and so on, leading up to finally hanging the drywall. Figure 5.4 offers an example of how an evidence-based lesson would look.

Planning and carrying out the lesson in such a way fully displays why various tasks connect with one another to complete the learning journey.

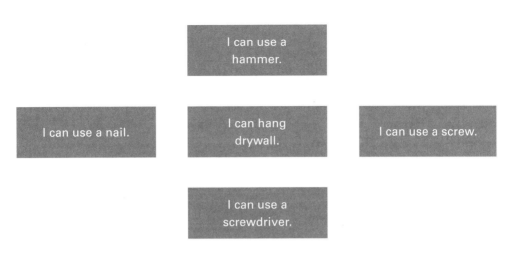

Figure 5.4: Learning targets in an evidence-based learning pathway.

Evidence-Based Grading Improves Team Collaboration

Perhaps the biggest change we have seen, thanks to evidence-based grading's implementation, is the way our teams and teachers collaborate. This change takes many forms, including (1) collaborative scoring, (2) fruitful conversations with and about students, (3) healthy dissonance, and (4) improved communication skills.

Collaborative Scoring

When teams have vetted their expectations, team members find it easier to rely on their colleagues for support on interpreting student performance (grading). As much as teachers collaborate, they still rarely entrust another teacher to help grade their students' work. This could be because of grading's personal nature. Most teachers don't vet learning targets together, outlining their collective expectations of student performance. When they do so, there is no reason they could not simply grade papers together or even trade student work and grade.

To highlight the need for this type of grading, think about how many times you have heard students say, "Oh, you have Mr. So-and-So and Ms. Whomever . . . they are such hard graders!" How does this happen? How can one teacher have a different expectation of quality than another teacher who teaches the same course? This simply should not happen, and it does not happen once teachers vet learning targets together. In our school, we have many evidence-based grading teams grade student performance together, with organized protocols in which one colleague grades performance and another compares the scores to historical data before they ultimately make a joint decision about a student's grade.

Fruitful Conversations With and About Students

A particularly impactful byproduct of an evidence-based grading system is dramatically improved conversations with and about students. Students and teachers use the language that describes the intended competency, which forces both parties to clearly discuss what they expect and what actually occurs. Without this engagement, students are often left with a misguided perspective on what they are expected to do, resulting in an expectation gap—the difference between what students believe teachers expect and what teachers actually expect.

Additionally, the teacher may be confused about why a student is not progressing. This can leave both parties thinking that the student simply needs more practice. This expectation gap prevents conversations in traditional classrooms from reaching their full potential. It's why giant review packets, rote practice, and study sessions still exist. Most traditional classroom teachers blame this disconnect on several factors, such as the lesson not being engaging enough, the student not paying attention, or the student just needing more practice. However, in our experience, it's usually little more than the teacher not using the language of what he or she expects in the learning target. When both parties use the target's language, the expectation gap narrows, and learning has the potential to move at a faster rate.

Healthy Dissonance

When teams collaboratively create performance expectations, vetting evidence and designing quality assessments simultaneously, a healthy dissonance may emerge. It comes from conversations that force team members to clearly articulate what they need from students, outline the best way to capture the evidence, and share their personal views about evidence. Often teams tackle each element separately, isolating any dissonance in a particular topic. In evidence-based grading, teams address each element simultaneously.

Improved Communication Skills

Teachers in evidence-based classrooms are usually better at communicating with students than those in traditional classrooms. This is because their communication focuses on how well they expect students to perform a skill or apply knowledge. This allows the student to gain a learning perspective that is unique to his or her own growth and ability.

Communication With the Community Is Essential

Communication with the community is a key aspect of evidence-based grading. Guskey and Jung (2013) state that evidence-based grading is "more about communicating better and [getting] more accurate information to families and students in order to provide the basis for improving student learning" (p. 119).

Before any change to the grading system is made, it is important to communicate with stakeholders about this change and the purpose behind it. If a school is merely reactive instead of proactive, it may become difficult for stakeholders to find value in the change. Similarly, implementation can stagnate if a school is too proactive and involves too many parties in the change. We must find the correct balance between early action and reaction.

Every time our school launches a new course with the new grading system, our staff send families a detailed letter outlining the importance of evidence-based grading. We changed our grading models course by course and team by team— we did not institutionalize this change in its full scale overnight. The letter we send explains evidence-based grading, why it is good for students, and how we calculate grades. Team leaders, administrators, and directors all sign the letter to show their support.

In evidence-based grading, the letter grade becomes less visible than with traditional grading. However, the fact remains that most students and families desire letter grades. In this system, we communicate about growth before giving letter grades. The community at large still does not accept evidence-based grading, so it is our job to help it see value in this system. Like one parent said, "I don't care if they can 'cite evidence from a text.' I care about two things—if my child is getting an A and if he is missing any assignments." Until our culture changes, we must continue giving letter grades. However, the culture *can* change if teachers give grades based on their interpretation of the evidence that students produce.

We Must Take a Postsecondary Perspective

We often hear from teachers and parents that colleges and universities don't seem to support this type of grading, so, they ask, shouldn't we model the same practices that they use in college? The fact remains that we still give letter grades, but will base them on evidence instead of on accumulated points. Evidence-based grading fosters for our students the essential ability to self-assess expectations. This is *the* skill that a student needs not only for college but also for the real world.

In the following sections, we look at how evidence-based grading supports postsecondary expectations.

Expectations and the Curious Case of A+

College admissions personnel and society as a whole tend to expect grade-A performance. They don't expect a B, as some teachers argue. In fact, one could argue that our true societal grading scale is A+, A, A–, and then everything else. In evidence-based grading, when we create proficiency-based learning targets and scales, we must ensure that stakeholders understand these nuances.

A 3 on the evidence-based scale *is* the expectation, with a 4 showing that the student has exceeded the expectation. A proficiency-based system needs to show that students can pass expectations; without that, the system becomes inequitable.

Transcripts

To ease the transition to evidence-based grading, we recommend leaving transcripts alone. In our school, we have the same GPA and same letter grades as traditional education systems. We simply base our grades, as we have stated before, on the *professional interpretation of the evidence*—nothing more, nothing less. While gradebooks are now based on learning targets and proficiency scores, transcripts remain unchanged. Through our gradebook technologies, we are able to offer much more clarity around student skill development, and we can communicate much more about what students know, understand, and can do. For this reason, transcripts can be much more effective in clarifying how well a student is progressing.

Figure 5.5 is an example of an evidence-based transcript. There are actually two evidence-based grading courses listed for this student, but it is impossible to tell which courses are evidence based and which are traditional. The information behind this transcript is very different, as shown in table 5.1.

Student and School Information		Grade Point Average Summary	
Student ID Number: 12345		Cumulative GPA (Weighted): 3.5000	
Birthday: 1/3/05		Cumulative GPA (Unweighted): 3.4118	
Counselor: Mr. Smith			
Guardian: Mr. and Mrs. Parent			
2012–2013 Grade 9 Semester One			
Course Completed		**Grade**	**Course Credit**
Mathematics 151: Geometry 1		B	1.0000 1
English 131: English Composition		A	1.0000 1
Science 111: Natural Science		B+	1.0000 1
Physical Education 104: Physical Education		P	1.0000 1
Social Science 134: World History		A	1.0000 1
Spanish 123: Spanish 3		A	1.0000 1
2012–2013 Grade 9 Semester Two			
Course Completed		**Grade**	**Course Credit**
Mathematics 151: Geometry 1		B	1.0000 1
English 131: English Composition		A	1.0000 1
Science 111: Natural Science		B+	1.0000 1
Physical Education 104: Physical Education		P	1.0000 1

| Social Science 134: World History | A | 1.0000 1 |
| Spanish 123: Spanish 3 | A | 1.0000 1 |

2013–2014 Grade 10 Semester One		
Course Completed	**Grade**	**Course Credit**
Mathematics 251: Algebra 2	B–	1.0000 1
English 331: English Literature	A	1.0000 1
Science 121: Biology	B	1.0000 1
Physical Education 174: Physical Education	P	1.0000 1
Social Science 154: U.S. History	A–	1.0000 1
Spanish 134: Spanish 4	C	1.0000 1

Figure 5.5: Transcript example for traditional and evidence-based courses.

Table 5.1: Information Behind Evidence-Based Transcript Grades

	Traditional Grading	**Evidence-Based Grading**
Grade on Transcript	A	A
Gradebook Level 1	93.4 percent	Interpersonal communication—4 Interpretive skills—4 Presentation communication—2
Gradebook Level 2	Homework—10 percent Participation—30 percent Quizzes and projects—20 percent Exams—40 percent	Learning target 1: Create meaning in a variety of contexts with minimal errors—4 Learning target 2: Identify cultural nuances in a variety of contexts—3
Gradebook Level 3	Homework—51/75 Participation—60/60 Quizzes and projects—79/102 Exams—345/532	Event 1 score—3 Event 2 score—2 Event 3 score—4
Gradebook Level 4	Quiz 1—30/40 Exam 1—45/50 Homework 1—3/5	

Notice that the information in the traditional course continues to focus on tasks and points as we go deeper into the student-grading structure, while the evidence-based grading structure focuses on proficiency scores with clear expectations. The evidence-based model leads to conversations about *learning* while the traditional model leads to conversations about *tasks*. The hierarchy in the right column always supports our transcript grades in evidence-based courses.

Seniors and Intermittent Grade Reporting

Colleges ask for intermittent grades for high school seniors. In evidence-based grading, the entire semester is open for learning. There are no term or quarter grades, just four months of feedback and learning per semester. This can be problematic for some colleges. As they review admissions, they may discover that they want or need an interim grade to support their admittance decision. We ask teachers of high school seniors to post a non-weighted grade at specified intervals throughout each semester to appease colleges.

Grade Inflation and Deflation

Grades are inflated in all grading systems, including evidence-based grading. This is because even in precise mathematical grading systems, teachers manipulate points to align with their perceptions of the student, those of the student for him- or herself, and especially those of the parent for the learner. These are the biases we must remove. Whether it is tweaking the points a little to make the percentage correct, making a test easier or harder based on the timing, or offering extra credit, the fact remains—grades in mathematical, traditional grading systems don't mean much.

On the other hand, giving students unreasonable expectations can deflate grades. Nitpicking nuances in the student's performance, failing to interpret the context of what the student intends in his or her work, and inconsistently applying points based on the time of submission or even the time of day that a teacher grades— these can all influence grades.

It is a myth that evidence-based grading inflates or deflates grades more than traditional grading systems. In our experience, we see that grade distributions are similar between the two. Table 5.2 shows the breakdown of grades in evidence-based courses and traditional courses in our 2013–2014 school year.

The fact remains that grades must represent only what a student's evidence shows. In the table, we see an increase in As not because evidence-based classes are easier, but because in evidence-based grading, teachers give students the grade that they truly deserve rather than what the points or computer systems say they deserve. Yes, we give more As, but that is because we have more students earning them. In essence, evidence-based grading gives more students a chance to be successful.

Table 5.2: Evidence-Based and Traditional Course Grade Distribution

	A	B	C	D	F
Evidence-Based Courses	54 percent	30 percent	14 percent	1 percent	1 percent
Traditional Courses	40 percent	40 percent	15 percent	4 percent	0 percent

Key Points

As our teacher teams get better at working with evidence-based grading, they become more and more observant about teaching and learning practices that reveal needed changes to curriculum, instruction, and assessment. In studying the evidence of student learning and examining the resulting data, our teacher teams are able to elaborate on successes and address concerns. This sustains a commitment to continuous improvement and recognizes collaboration's value. Review the following key points from this chapter to ensure that you firmly grasp the content.

- Teachers assign grades based on their interpretation of the evidence.

- Collaboration is different in an evidence-based grading system than in a traditional grading system.

- A postsecondary perspective is important for an evidence-based grading system to work.

Epilogue

With every passing day, we become more confident in our efforts to reform traditional grading practices. Since 2012, we've worked to make the change to an evidence-based grading model, and throughout that time, we've gathered more and more positive and powerful examples of successes in teaching and learning.

One of our colleagues received an email from her child's German teacher in a neighboring school. It stated that her child, Matthew, had received a 72 percent on the chapter test. It went on to explain that the grade had nothing to do with Matthew's understanding of the material and also didn't reflect his ability or great work ethic. His teacher emphasized that Matthew was a very hard worker.

Here's our thought: If the grade had nothing to do with Matthew's understanding of the material, then why did he get that grade? If the grade of 72 percent was not an accurate, fair, and effective representation of Matthew's learning and understanding, then what did it represent? Did it represent effort? It clearly did not, as the teacher stated that the grade did not reflect Matthew's work ethic. Did the grade reflect improvement? It didn't seem to, as the teacher acknowledged that Matthew's mistakes did not reflect his ability.

In the end, the grade of 72 percent represents nothing more than simple arithmetic in which the teacher divided the points earned on the test by the points possible and computed a score—an average. This is the same way teachers have computed grades for years. We know that calculating grades this way isn't effective. We must improve the way we communicate about student learning and performance. An arbitrary number says very little compared to the descriptive feedback of an evidence-based grading model.

As we travel down the path of evidence-based grading, we are reminded over and over again that we are on the right path toward building clarity in how we communicate about teaching and learning. More important, students are benefiting as a result.

Another email exchange took place in the fall of 2015 between one of our curriculum directors and a student who was in a class where the teacher used evidence-based grading. This student stated, "I really like the way Mrs. Farkas teaches; she makes it easy to understand. To be quite honest, I didn't really work that hard. I thank evidence-based grading for that!"

When the curriculum director asked the student what she meant by "not working that hard," the student responded:

> Evidence-based grading makes it easier in a sense that it bunches things together compared to our normal grading. It's easy for me to see what I'm struggling with. The feedback really points out what I need to work on. . . . It allows my teacher to guide me to the correct answer. I feel like students would really appreciate knowing exactly where they stand with their grades, and what specifically they need to improve on. (A. Miller, personal communication, March 12, 2013)

This kind of email from a student is very exciting! We know that we are making significant progress when students are able to clearly articulate the benefits and value of our changes in grading. It's obvious that this student received effective feedback that enabled her to make adjustments and improvements in her learning and understanding. Grades can be effective instructional and feedback tools when we don't use them to sort and rank students but instead give them to students as meaningful information about their progress toward learning targets and expectations.

It is not just students who give us positive feedback on evidence-based grading. Given that we have more than 150 different curriculum teams in our building, we have chosen not to mandate that all teams implement evidence-based grading at the same time. Instead, we decided to facilitate each team's journey to evidence-based grading through the creative process we have outlined in this book (preparation, incubation, insight, evaluation, and elaboration). As a result, while we have most teachers working in evidence-based grading curriculum teams, we do have some teachers who are still in the preparation phase and have not yet made the full switch.

We once received a phone call that demonstrated to us that we are definitely on the right path. The call came from the mother of a freshman who had experienced evidence-based grading practices throughout his elementary and middle school years. Most of her son's teachers used evidence-based grading, but one did not. In that one class, the teacher continued to use the traditional one-hundred-point percentage system that determined the grade by dividing total points earned by total points possible.

After this student received his first test back in September with a grade of 82 percent, he and his mother were utterly confused. She called the teacher, the department chair, and the principal, trying to figure out exactly what the grade meant. The mother asked, "What does an 82 percent mean? I don't understand what a B is really telling me about my son's understanding of the targets. Can someone just give us feedback that will tell my son what he needs to know and improve?"

Of course, everything this parent said is true. It was her last question, however, that affirmed our work and convinced us that there is no turning back to traditional grading practices. Traditional grading practices express very little. They explain nothing about learning in any specific, direct, and articulated way. An evidence-based grading model demands clarity. It informs learning and creates a mindset of continuous growth and improvement. As we work with this model, we are seeing a greater level of coherence within the relationship among curriculum, instruction, and assessment. Likewise, our students are more connected to meaningful learning experiences that point them in a direction of growth.

We are excited to share this work and the way that we continue to question and advance conversations about teaching and learning. As we press forward with other positive changes in education, we are proud that our grading practices are starting to reflect our values and beliefs about teaching and learning. We hope other schools jump on board with building this reform in grading practices, and we hope you will reach out to us and provide us with your insights, thoughts, and ideas about evidence-based grading. Let's collaborate!

References and Resources

Adair-Hauck, B., Glisan, E. W., & Troyan, F. J. (2013). *Implementing integrated performance assessment*. Alexandria, VA: American Council on the Teaching of Foreign Languages.

Ainsworth, L., & Viegut, D. (2006). *Common formative assessments: How to connect standards-based instruction and assessment*. Thousand Oaks, CA: Corwin Press.

Amabile, T. M. (1983). *The social psychology of creativity*. New York: Springer-Verlag.

Barnes, M. (2015). *Assessment 3.0: Throw out your grade book and inspire learning*. Thousand Oaks, CA: Corwin Press.

Black, P., & Wiliam, D. (1998). *Inside the black box: Raising standards through classroom assessment*. London: King's College.

Brimi, H. M. (2011). Reliability of grading high school work in English. *Practical Assessment, Research and Evaluation, 16*(17), 1–12.

Brown, P. C., Roediger, H. L., III, & McDaniel, M. A. (2014). *Make it stick: The science of successful learning*. Cambridge, MA: Belknap Press of Harvard University Press.

Buehl, D. (2011). *Developing readers in the academic disciplines*. Newark, DE: International Reading Association.

Buffum, A., Mattos, M., & Weber, C. (2012). *Simplifying response to intervention: Four essential guiding principles*. Bloomington, IN: Solution Tree Press.

Burke, K. (1999). *How to assess authentic learning* (3rd ed.). Arlington Heights, IL: Skylight.

Chappuis, J. (2009). *Seven strategies of assessment for learning*. Portland, OR: Educational Testing Service.

Collins, J. (2001). *Good to great: Why some companies make the leap . . . and others don't*. New York: HarperBusiness.

Csikszentmihalyi, M. (1990). *Flow: The psychology of optimal experience*. New York: Harper & Row.

Danielson, C. (2007). *Enhancing professional practice: A framework for teaching* (2nd ed.). Alexandria, VA: Association for Supervision and Curriculum Development.

Danielson, C. (2013). *The framework for teaching evaluation instrument* (2013 ed.). Princeton, NJ: Danielson Group. Accessed at www.teachscape.com/binaries /content/assets/teachscape-marketing-website/products/ffteval/2013-framework -for-teaching-evaluation-instrument.pdf on January 5, 2016.

Dueck, M. (2014). *Grading smarter, not harder: Assessment strategies that motivate kids and help them learn*. Alexandria, VA: Association for Supervision and Curriculum Development.

Durm, M. W. (1993). An A is not an A: A history of grading. *The Educational Forum, 57*(3), 294–297.

Elbaum, D. (2015, May). The A.C.T. explorer reading model: Combining formative assessment and reading strategies. *The Assessor, 3*.

Elder, D. (2012). *Standard based teaching: A classroom guide*. Scotts Valley, CA: CreateSpace.

Evidence. (n.d.). In *Merriam-Webster's online dictionary*. Accessed at www.merriam -webster.com/dictionary/evidence on November 7, 2016.

Flower, L. (1981). *Problem-solving strategies for writing*. New York: Harcourt Brace Jovanovich.

Gobble, T., Onuscheck, M., Reibel, A. R., & Twadell, E. (2016). *Proficiency-based assessment: Process, not product*. Bloomington, IN: Solution Tree Press.

Gregory, K., Cameron, C., & Davies, A. (2011). *Self-assessment and goal setting* (2nd ed.). Bloomington, IN: Solution Tree Press.

Guo, K. (2015, February 27). What happens when students rent learning? *Statesman*. Accessed at www.statesmanshs.org/1055/features/what-happens-when-students -rent-learning on January 13, 2016.

Guskey, T. R. (2013). The case against percentage grades. *Educational Leadership, 71*(1), 68–72.

Guskey, T. R. (2015). *On your mark: Challenging the conventions of grading and reporting*. Bloomington, IN: Solution Tree Press.

Guskey, T. R., & Bailey, J. M. (2001). *Developing grading and reporting systems for student learning*. Thousand Oaks, CA: Corwin Press.

Guskey, T. R., & Jung, L. A. (2013). *Answers to essential questions about standards, assessments, grading, and reporting*. Thousand Oaks, CA: Corwin Press.

Heflebower, T., Hoegh, J. K., & Warrick, P. (2014). *A school leader's guide to standards-based grading*. Bloomington, IN: Marzano Research.

Kendall, J. S., & Marzano, R. J. (1997). *Content knowledge: A compendium of standards and benchmarks for K–12 education* (2nd ed.). Aurora, CO: McREL.

Kohn, A. (2006). *The homework myth: Why our kids get too much of a bad thing*. Cambridge, MA: Da Capo Life Long.

Lillydahl, D. (2012, August 24). *Parent communication* [Letter to parents of students]. Adlai E. Stevenson High School, Lincolnshire, IL.

Lipton, L., & Wellman, B. (2011). *Groups at work: Strategies and structures for professional learning*. Charlotte, NC: MiraVia.

Martinez, M., & Reibel, A. (2015, May). Re-assessment vs. re-evaluation. *The Assessor*, 5.

Marzano, R. J. (2003). *What works in schools: Translating research into action*. Alexandria, VA: Association for Supervision and Curriculum Development.

Marzano, R. J. (2006). *Classroom assessment and grading that work*. Alexandria, VA: Association for Supervision and Curriculum Development.

Marzano, R. J. (2009). *Designing and teaching learning goals and objectives*. Bloomington, IN: Marzano Research.

McTighe, J., & Ferrara, S. (2000). *Assessing learning in the classroom*. Washington, DC: National Education Association.

Moss, C. M., & Brookhart, S. M. (2012). *Learning targets: Helping students aim for understanding in today's lesson*. Alexandria, VA: Association for Supervision and Curriculum Development.

O'Connor, K. (2007a). The last frontier: Tackling the grading dilemma. In D. Reeves (Ed.), *Ahead of the curve: The power of assessment to transform teaching and learning* (pp. 127–146). Bloomington, IN: Solution Tree Press.

O'Connor, K. (2007b). *A repair kit for grading: 15 fixes for broken grades*. Portland, OR: Educational Testing Service.

O'Connor, K. (2009). *How to grade for learning, K–12* (3rd ed.). Thousand Oaks, CA: Corwin Press.

O'Connor, K. (2011). *A repair kit for grading: 15 fixes for broken grades* (2nd ed.). Boston: Pearson.

Olson, L. (1995). Cards on the table. *Education Week*, *15*(41), 23–28.

Reeves, D. (Ed.). (2007). *Ahead of the curve: The power of assessment to transform teaching and learning*. Bloomington, IN: Solution Tree Press.

Reeves, D. (2008). Leading to change / Effective grading practices. *Educational Leadership*, *65*(5), 85–87.

Reeves, D. (2016a). *Elements of grading: A guide to effective practice* (2nd ed.). Bloomington, IN: Solution Tree Press.

Reeves, D. (2016b). *FAST grading: A guide to implementing best practices*. Bloomington, IN: Solution Tree Press.

Ripley, A. (2013). *The smartest kids in the world: And how they got that way*. New York: Simon & Schuster.

Ritchhart, R., Church, M., & Morrison, K. (2011). *Making thinking visible: How to promote engagement, understanding, and independence for all learners*. San Francisco: Jossey-Bass.

Sandrock, P. (2011, December 8). *Designing backwards: From performance assessments to units of instruction*. Lecture conducted at the American Council on the Teaching of Foreign Languages, Lincolnshire, IL.

Savage, S. L. (2012). *The flaw of averages: Why we underestimate risk in the face of uncertainty*. Hoboken, NJ: Wiley.

Schoemaker, P. J. H. (2011). *Brilliant mistakes: Finding success on the far side of failure* [E-reader version]. Philadelphia: Wharton Digital Press.

Schulze, H. (2015, August 12). Session 5: Creating world class service. Session conducted at the Global Leadership Summit, Barrington, IL.

Sperling, D. (1993). What's worth an "A"? Setting standards together. *Educational Leadership, 50*(5), 73–75.

Starch, D., & Elliott, E. C. (1912). Reliability of the grading of high-school work in English. *School Review, 20*(7), 442–457.

Stiggins, R. (2006). Assessment *for* learning: A key to motivation and achievement. *EDge, 2*(2), 3–19.

Stiggins, R., Arter, J., Chappuis, J., & Chappuis, S. (2004). *Classroom assessment for student learning: Doing it right—using it well.* Portland, OR: Assessment Training Institute.

Stiggins, R., & Chappuis, J. (2008). Enhancing student learning. *District Administration, 44*(1), 42–44.

Tovani, C. (2012). Feedback is a two-way street. *Educational Leadership, 70*(1), 48–51.

University of Illinois at Urbana–Champaign. (2014). *Illinois youth survey: Survey results.* Accessed at https://iys.cprd.illinois.edu/results on January 14, 2016.

Vatterott, C. (2009). *Rethinking homework: Best practices that support diverse needs.* Alexandria, VA: Association for Supervision and Curriculum Development.

Vatterott, C. (2015). *Rethinking grading: Meaningful assessment for standards-based learning.* Alexandria, VA: Association for Supervision and Curriculum Development.

Wiggins, G. (1996). Honesty and fairness: Toward better grading and reporting. In T. R. Guskey (Ed.), *Communicating student learning: The 1996 ASCD yearbook* (pp. 141–177). Alexandria, VA: Association for Supervision and Curriculum Development.

Wiggins, G. (1998). *Educative assessment: Designing assessments to inform and improve student performance.* San Francisco: Jossey-Bass.

Wiggins, G. (2010, May 22). *Feedback: How learning occurs.* Accessed at www .authenticeducation.org/bigideas/article.lasso?artid=61 on June 20, 2015.

Wiggins, G., & McTighe, J. (2005). *Understanding by design* (Expanded 2nd ed.). Alexandria, VA: Association for Supervision and Curriculum Development.

Wiliam, D. (2011). *Embedded formative assessment.* Bloomington, IN: Solution Tree Press.

Willis, S. (1993). Are letter grades obsolete? *Education Update, 35*(7), 4–8.

Wormeli, R. (2014, November 12). *Standards-based assessment and grading.* Lecture conducted at the Illinois Association for Supervision and Curriculum Development's Curriculum 2020, DeKalb, IL.

Zizzo, J. (2015, November). Us vs. them: For whom is the feedback, anyway? *The Assessor,* 15.

Index

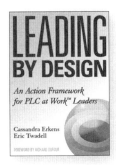

Leading by Design
Cassandra Erkens and Eric Twadell
After interviewing and observing principals, administrators, and teachers, the authors identify seven leadership practices that effective PLC leaders share, along with the techniques that have led them to sustainable success.
BKF430

Proficiency-Based Assessment
Troy Gobble, Mark Onuscheck, Anthony R. Reibel, and Eric Twadell
With this resource, teachers will discover how to close the gaps between assessment, curriculum, and instruction by replacing outmoded assessment methods with proficiency-based assessments. Learn the essentials of proficiency-based assessment, and explore evidence-based strategies for successful implementation.
BKF631

On Your Mark
Thomas R. Guskey
Create and sustain a learning environment where students thrive and stakeholders are accurately informed of student progress. Clarify the purpose of grades, craft a vision statement aligned with this purpose, and discover research-based strategies to implement effective grading and reporting practices.
BKF606

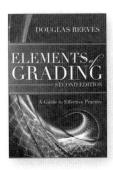

Elements of Grading, Second Edition
Douglas Reeves
The author provides educators with practical suggestions for making the grading process more fair, accurate, specific, and timely. In addition to examples and case studies, new content addresses how the Common Core State Standards and new technologies impact grading practices.
BKF648